PSALMS AND PRAYER

31 INSIGHTS FROM A.W. PINK, C.H. SPURGEON, THOMAS WATSON, JOHN CALVIN, MATTHEW HENRY, AND MORE.

GODLIPRESS TEAM

© Copyright 2022 by GodliPress. All rights reserved.

This book is copyright protected. You cannot amend, distribute, sell, use, quote or paraphrase any part, or the content within this book, without the consent of the author or publisher, except in the case of brief quotations embodied in critical articles or reviews.

Scripture quotations are from The ESV® Bible (The Holy Bible, English Standard Version®), copyright © 2001 by Crossway, a publishing ministry of Good News Publishers. Used by permission. All rights reserved.

CONTENTS

Introduction	vii
1. PSALM 102 - HEAR MY CRY	1
God's Hearing	2
Our Crying	3
Daily Reflections	4
2. PSALM 51 - PRAYING FOR A CLEAN HEART	5
Daily Reflections	8
3. PSALM 32 - CONFESSING SINS	10
Daily Reflections	13
4. PSALM 20 - A PRAYER FOR THOSE IN AUTHORITY	15
Daily Reflections	18
5. PSALM 20 - PRAYING WITH CONFIDENCE FOR OTHERS	20
Daily Reflections	23
6. PSALM 36 - A PRAYER FOR MERCY AND JUSTICE	24
Daily Reflections	27
7. PSALM 37 - WAITING ON GOD	28
Daily Reflections	31
8. PSALM 119 - YOU HAVE HEARD ME	33
Daily Reflections	36
9. PSALM 112 - A FIRM HEART TO PRAY	37
Not Afraid	37
Trusting	38
Daily Reflections	40
10. PSALM 23 - WHO CAN HEAR HIS VOICE?	41
The Conditions	43
Daily Reflections	44

11. PSALM 10 - DAVID PLEADS HIS CASE	45
Daily Reflections	47
12. PSALM 123 - LIFTING UP OUR EYES	49
Daily Reflections	53
13. PSALM 123 - HAVE MERCY ON US	54
Daily Reflections	57
14. PSALM 27 - ONE THING I ASKED FOR	58
Praying for Clarity	59
Seeking Spiritual Things	60
Daily Reflections	61
15. PSALM 122 - PRAY FOR THE CHURCH	62
Daily Reflections	65
16. PSALM 46 - BE STILL	66
Daily Reflections	69
17. PSALM 40 - GOD ANSWERS IN TRIALS	70
Daily Reflections	73
18. PSALM 119 - A PRAYER FOR COMFORT	74
The Source of Comfort	75
God Wants Us to Ask	76
Daily Reflections	77
19. PSALM 42 - PRAYING IN DIFFICULTIES	78
The Dark, Cloudy Day	78
The Hour of Temptation	79
Self-Occupation	79
Daily Reflections	81
20. PSALM 25 - LEARNING TO WAIT IN PRAYER	82
Daily Reflections	85
21. PSALM 84 - ONE DAY IN YOUR COURTS	86
Daily Reflections	89
22. PSALM 119 - NOT JUST A DUTY	90
Daily Reflections	93

23. PSALM 119 - PRIVATE PRAYER	94
David's Example	95
Daily Reflections	97
24. PSALM 6 - PATIENCE IN PRAYER	98
Waiting as God Does	100
Daily Reflections	101
25. PSALM 141 - GUARD MY TONGUE	103
Daily Reflections	106
26. PSALM 124 - THANKSGIVING FOR BEING SAVED	107
God Saves and Protects	108
Daily Reflections	110
27. PSALM 119 - THE WAY IS OPEN FOR PRAYER	112
Daily Reflections	115
28. PSALM 28 - THANKS, DECLARATION, AND PETITION	116
Daily Reflections	119
29. PSALM 17 - A PRAYER TO BE HEARD	121
Daily Reflections	123
30. PSALM 119 - GRATITUDE FOR HIS GOODNESS	125
Daily Reflections	128
31. PSALM 131 - PRAYING FOR HUMILITY	129
Humility Through Hardship	131
A Secret to Learn	132
Daily Reflections	133
About the Authors	135
Bibliography	143

INTRODUCTION

Ask any Christian for their favorite verses in the Bible and they will undoubtedly have one from Psalms somewhere in their list. Some of the most loved and well-known scriptures in and outside of the church are found in this anthology.

It is no wonder that at one time, they were thought of as the only true way to worship and express yourself to God. Churches were forbidden from any hymns that did not use the words of the Psalms, and it took great courage for Isaac Watts to break from tradition and seek inspiration from the New Testament.

The Psalms is a special book and is probably one of the most read in terms of inspiration when people are searching for personal answers or are unsure of how to form their own words toward God. In trouble and triumph, this collection of songs and poems reflects an honesty that we can all relate to.

Not just praise and thanksgiving, the many heartfelt and honest responses and prayers to God resonate with us because we also go through hardships, times of despair, or even doubt. And in these, we can learn some truths about the way David was able to approach God so openly.

Drawing from some of the classic Christian writers of centuries ago, we have put together a selection of their insights into different Psalms, specifically looking at prayer. These authors are all known for their solid faith and doctrinal views, and what they share can encourage and challenge you in your own prayer life.

By bringing their timeless words into modern English, we have been careful not to lose any of the rich meaning that they describe in these Psalms, so that you may benefit as much as if you were reading this a few hundred years ago. Using a 31-day format, this book becomes accessible as a daily devotion, with extra reflective questions that will make you think more about each passage.

More and more, we should have prayers that resemble those found in the book of Psalms, because there is a spiritual depth there that we often miss in our superficial modern language. Praying along the same lines as David, and understanding his heart before God, we can only grow closer to God in communion with Him. Then, as in 1 Corinthians 14:26, we will be able to bring a psalm, a song, or a prayer with us when we are in church.

Let your thoughts be psalms, your prayers incense, and your breath praise. –Charles Spurgeon

1

PSALM 102 - HEAR MY CRY

Hear my prayer, O Lord;
let my cry come to you!
Do not hide your face from me
in the day of my distress!
Incline your ear to me;
answer me speedily in the day when I call!
Psalm 102:1-2

If praying is a pleasing thing to God, why must we pray that he will hear our prayer? Is prayer not a tribute due to God, and does the subject have to pray that the prince will receive his tribute? Is prayer not a sacrifice that is proper to God, and will he not accept the smoke of it, if it is suitable? But what if it is not a prayer unless God hears it, a tribute unless he receives it, or a sacrifice unless he smells a sweet scent in it? If God does not hear it, it is not a prayer but a useless speech. If God does not receive it, it is not a tribute but a vain expense. If God does not smell a sweet smell in it, it is not a sacrifice that makes fire, but no smoke that can ascend to heaven. Is this not enough reason to say, *"Hear my prayer, O Lord; let my cry come to you!"*?

Is it an inferior thing for God, who lives in the heavens, to hear your prayer, a worm crawling on the earth? Is God not the great Ruler and Governor of all things, and is beneath him, in the midst of his infinite duties, to leave them all, and to stand listening to you? *"What is man that you are mindful of him, and the son of man that you care for him?"* (Psalm 8:4). Did he not make him lower than the angels with whom he converses and whom he always hears? Lower in all other things, except in prayer.

God's Hearing

But can I make a prayer to God that he does not hear? Why do I need to pray that he will hear that which I am sure he hears without asking him to hear it? I know, O God, you hear the young ravens that call on you, but such hearing is from your general provision and falls like the rain on the just and unjust. The hearing I need is in your mercy, and in your mercy, I humbly beg you to hear my prayer and to let my cry come to you. I do not need you to hear me excusing myself as Adam did in the garden. I do not ask you to hear me justifying myself as Saul did to Samuel. I do not require you only to hear me praying humbly as the tax collector did, but I hope you will see fit to hear and to let my cry come to you. I know you do not hear as men do; they hear a supplication but do not regard it, or they hear it but are not able to help.

Your hearing is always with a will to act, with a power to effect. With this kind of hearing, I humbly beg you to hear my prayer and let my cry come to you. But if my praying should not succeed, then I raise it to a cry because crying is the greatest bell in all the rings of praying—there is nothing louder than crying in prayer. If not my prayer, at least let my cry come to you.

Our Crying

But what is this cry? Is it just the voice speaking loudly? Let me leave this loudness to the priests of Baal who cry to their gods that have ears but cannot hear. My God hears the loudness of the heart and can hear a cry in Hannah's prayer when Eli hears nothing but her lips are moving. He can hear a cry in Moses' prayer when no one heard him speak a word. If I am not heard when I cry, I will cry for not being heard, and if I am heard when I cry, I will cry to be heard. So, whether I am heard or not heard, I will still cry, and if he lets me cry, may he hear my prayer, and let my cry come to him.

But it is not so much the loudness of my crying that God regards as humility and strength. Even though we can pray with reservation, we can never cry without submission. Even though prayer can be faint and weak, crying is always vigorous and strong. But as humble as it is, it must not come to him without permission, and as strong as it is, it cannot come to him without assistance.

Then let my cry come to you, O God; let it come both permissively and effectively, that having your consent and your assistance it may come to you, not only with boldness but with assurance—with boldness as having your leave, and with assurance as having your assistance. Without your assistance, it cannot come to you; it will either stay groveling with worldly desires or hover in the air with ambitious thoughts and never be able to ascend to you. But if by your grace you listen to my cry, it will then break through the clouds and will pierce the heavens, and nothing will be able to stop it from coming to you.

Richard Baker

(Baker, 1640)

Daily Reflections

Prayer is all about speaking, listening, and hearing. Sometimes, we feel like it is one-way traffic, or we feel like it is just speaking into the wind and that God is hiding from us. This Psalm carries many of those same feelings, and we can identify with the words.

1. Have you ever felt God is not listening to you? Why?
2. What kind of hearing does Baker insist we ask God for?
3. Have you ever cried to God—a broken, desperate call to Him to meet your need? Why do you think God wants us to cry to Him?

2

PSALM 51 - PRAYING FOR A CLEAN HEART

Create in me a clean heart, O God,
and renew a right spirit within me
Psalm 51:10

In a verse before this, David prayed, *"Purge me with hyssop, and I shall be clean"* (Psalm 51:7). A person becomes clean when they are sprinkled with the blood of Jesus and are purged and acquitted from their sin. Now, David prays again to be made clean, but it happens in another way. He prays that the Lord may create within him a clean heart—make a new heart for him that is clean by His divine power.

There are two ways in which the unclean can become clean before God. The one is when he is washed and cleansed from his guilt in the blood of Jesus, judicially acquitted. The other, when he is renewed and inwardly changed, receives a new and clean heart in place of the old and unclean. To understand the way of salvation, the work of grace, and the prayer for grace aright, we must understand this two-fold purity.

The first is when the soul becomes acquitted by the blood of Jesus. When God throws sin behind His back, a person is entirely freed from the guilt that is resting on them, and they are judicially clean—they have fulfilled the demands of the law and paid their guilt, either by themselves or by another as a guarantee. In that case, the law demands nothing more from me. I stand guiltless and clean. The law only asks about what I have done and what I have been, not about what I still am or what I am going to do.

So, a judge on earth can acquit or pronounce clean without implying that the heart of the acquitted man is clean, or that he is beyond the possibility of committing the same sin again. Even though God knows that the heart is inwardly impure, the sinner is pronounced clean by the law as soon as all the demands of the law are fulfilled. The demands of the law have been fulfilled by the precious Savior, by His obedience and His suffering, and therefore, is pronounced clean in His blood. This is the purity that David has spoken of in the first half of the Psalm, the complete forgiveness of sins, being made *"whiter than snow."*

But this purity is not all that he needs. There is a second cleanness, the fruit, and the consequence of the first. An earthly judge can acquit a person or pronounce them clean although their hearts still continue to follow their sins, and he may go from the court to commit them again. But God does not do this. He acquits the sinner and pronounces him clean only for Jesus' sake but does not leave him like that. As soon as He acquits him, He begins the work of inner purification. The very same grace which teaches us to pray for the first purity, the judicial cleansing from the acquittal of the law teaches us to also desire the second purity, the inner cleansing that comes through the renewing of the Spirit. That is why David carries on to pray *"Create in me a clean heart, O God."* The one is as indispensable as the other—the two are one. They are two different ways that the purity of Jesus comes to us. As soon as we believe, the righteousness of Christ is ours, and we are immediately clean, but the inner purity of Jesus to the soul takes place in stages.

These two are one, but they should not be mixed up together. The one cleanness is a root, the other is a fruit. The one goes first, and the other follows after. David has first prayed for the one in verses 8-9, then he asks for the other. And, pray, never forget that the first, the cleansing of the blood of Christ, is given before you can inwardly receive the second, and that only he who receives and accepts the first shall have the power to obtain the second.

Let it be your prayer, *"Have mercy on me, O God… blot out my transgressions… create in me a clean heart"* (Psalm 51:1-10). May God teach us to offer up this prayer with deep sincerity and with our whole hearts.

The desire of the true supplicant strives for inner purity. David was not content with simply praying for the forgiveness of his transgressions. No, he felt that his whole nature was inwardly corrupt. He desired also to be inwardly purified. He was not content simply with acquittal from merited punishment. But many of us are quite content with this. No, he desired to also be free from the power and indwelling of sin. He desired to be holy and not sin anymore.

This clean heart must also be your expectation. God the Creator is also God the Renewer. He can do this. As the work of the first creation was not completed at once but step by step, so also will it be with the renewal. God can perform this work. He can make the unclean heart clean. This is what grace will do for you. Let your expectation reach out to this blessing. When you pray for forgiveness, let it only be as a step to becoming holy. God is pure, God is holy, and no prayer will be more welcome to Him than that He should make you holy also. *"Create in me a clean heart, O God."*

Andrew Murray

(Murray, 2015)

Daily Reflections

Murray opens this Psalm to show a critical part of our Christianity—coming to God for a clean heart. He reveals that there is not just one type of cleanliness but a second, deeper one, beyond just having our sins forgiven. This prayer shows an incredible desire for holiness.

1. What is the difference between the first and the second clean heart that is spoken of here?

2. Read Psalm 24:4 and James 4:8. How do these relate to our reading?
3. Have you ever prayed for a clean heart?

3
PSALM 32 - CONFESSING SINS

For when I kept silent, my bones wasted away
through my groaning all day long.
For day and night your hand was heavy upon me;
my strength was dried up as by the heat of summer. Selah
I acknowledged my sin to you,
and I did not cover my iniquity;
I said, "I will confess my transgressions to the Lord,"
and you forgave the iniquity of my sin. Selah
Therefore let everyone who is godly
offer prayer to you at a time when you may be found
Psalm 32:3-6

David tells us about his own experience. No instructor is so efficient as one who testifies to what he has personally known and felt.

"For when I kept silent." When I failed to confess, or in despair dared not do so, my bones became old and began to decay with weakness, because my grief was so intense that it sapped my health and destroyed my vital energy. What a killing thing is sin! It is a pestilent disease! A fire in the bones! While we smother our sin, it rages within, and like a wound swells and torments.

"Through my groaning all day long." He was silent when it came to confession, but not with his sorrow. Horrified by his guilt, David cried until his voice was no longer like normal speech, but so much sighing and groaning that it resembled the roaring of a wounded beast.

No one knows the pain of conviction except those who have endured them. Rather suffer all the diseases of the body than the crushing judgment of almighty God. The Spanish Inquisition with all its tortures was nothing to the inquest that the conscience holds within the heart.

"For day and night your hand was heavy upon me." If God's finger can crush us, what must his hand feel like, pressing heavily and continuously? God's hand is very helpful when it uplifts, but it is awful when it presses down. Rather a world on the shoulder, like Atlas—than God's hand on the heart, like David.

"My strength was dried up as by the heat of summer." The sap of his soul was dry and his body appeared to be without its necessary fluids. The oil was almost gone from the lamp of life, and the flame flickered as though it would soon expire. Unconfessed transgression, like a fierce poison, dried up the fountain of David's strength and made him like a tree blasted

by the lightning, or a plant withered by the scorching heat of a tropical sun. What a poor soul that has learned its sin but forgets its Savior.

"I acknowledged my sin to you." After waiting a long time, the broken heart decided to do what it should have done in the first place and exposed itself before the Lord. The scalpel must be allowed into the growing ulcer before relief can come. The least we can do, if we want to be forgiven, is to acknowledge our fault. If we are too proud to do this, we double deserve punishment!

"And I did not cover my iniquity." We must confess the guilt as well as the sin. It is useless to hide it, for it is already known to God. It is beneficial for us to own it because a full confession softens and humbles the heart. We must uncover the secrets of the soul, dig up the hidden treasure of Achan, by bringing out our sins.

"I said." This was his determined decision.

"I will confess my transgressions to the Lord." Not to other people or the high priest, but to Jehovah. Even in those days of symbols, the faithful looked to God alone for deliverance from sin's heavy load—even more so now, when we no longer need representations. When the heart decides to lay low and plead guilty, absolution is near. So, we read, *"and you forgave the iniquity of my sin."*

Not only was the sin forgiven, but the iniquity of it. The virus of its guilt was put away as soon as the acknowledgment was made. God's pardons are deep and thorough. The knife of mercy cuts at the roots of the evil weed of sin.

"Therefore let everyone who is godly offer prayer to you at a time when you may be found." Remarkable answers to prayer motivate the prayerfulness of other godly people. Where one man finds a golden nugget, others feel inclined to dig. The benefit of our experience to others should reconcile us to it. Perhaps the Psalmist meant for all to draw near to God in the same way he did when godliness rules their heart. The mercy seat is the way to Heaven for all who come there.

There is, however, a set time for prayer, after which it will be unavailable. Between the time of sin and the day of punishment, there is mercy, and God may be found. But when the sentence has been handed down, pleading will be useless, because the Lord will not be found by the condemned soul.

Do not waste the day of salvation. The righteous pray, while the Lord has promised to answer—the ungodly postpone their petitions until the Master of the house has got up and shut the door, and then their knocking is too late.

Charles Spurgeon

(Grace Gems, 2022)

Daily Reflections

Sin can eat us up and even cause us to become ill unless we admit our wrongs to God and come before Him in repentance. Honesty and vulnerability before God are what He admired most about David, and we can see that in this Psalm. Sometimes, we need to be real about the state of our hearts rather than leaving it or covering it up.

1. Have you ever felt, like David, that unless you confess your sins, they will consume you?
2. Do you sometimes wait until it is almost too late to confess? Why?
3. Why does Spurgeon say, "We must confess the guilt as well as the sin"?
4. What does it mean that there is a certain time given between mercy and judgment for us to confess?

4

PSALM 20 - A PRAYER FOR THOSE IN AUTHORITY

May the Lord answer you in the day of trouble!
May the name of the God of Jacob protect you!
May he send you help from the sanctuary
and give you support from Zion!
May he remember all your offerings
and regard with favor your burnt sacrifices! Selah
May he grant you your heart's desire
and fulfill all your plans!
May we shout for joy over your salvation,
and in the name of our God set up our banners!
May the Lord fulfill all your petitions!
Psalm 20:1-5

It is the will of God that prayers, intercessions, and thanksgivings should be made for those in authority.

This prayer for David is called a Psalm of David. It was not strange for him to write a form of prayer to be used in the congregation for himself and those in authority under him. It is right for those who desire the prayers of their friends to tell them specifically what they want God to be asked of them. Even great and good men pray for themselves and should desire the prayers of others for them, even those who are beneath them. Paul often begged his friends to pray for him. Magistrates and those in power should encourage praying people, to see their strength (Zec. 12:5, 10), and to do what they can for them, so that they may have an interest in their prayers.

What should we pray for the person in authority?

1. That God would answer His prayers: *"May the Lord answer you in the day of trouble!"* (v. 1), and the Lord fulfill all your requests, v. 5. Even the greatest of men may be much in trouble. It was often a day of trouble for David, full of disappointment, distress, and confusion. Neither the crown on his head nor the grace in his heart would exempt him from the trouble. Even the greatest of men must be in prayer. David, though a man of business and a man of war, was constant in his devotions. He had prophets, priests, and many good people to pray for him, but he did not think that excused him from praying for himself. Let none expect to benefit by the prayers of

the church, or of their ministers or friends for them, who are capable of praying for themselves, and yet they neglect it. The prayers of others for us must be desired, not to supersede but to supplement our own for ourselves.

2. That God would protect him and preserve his life in times of war: *"May the name of the God of Jacob protect you!"* (v. 1). David had mighty men for his guards, but he commits himself, and his people also commit him, to the care of God. "Let God by his grace keep thee easy from the fear of evil. *"The name of the Lord is a strong tower; the righteous man runs into it and is safe"* (Prov. 18:10). May those in authority be able to shelter themselves in that strong tower.

3. That God would enable him to carry on in his undertakings for the public good—that in the day of battle God would send him help out of the sanctuary, and strength out of Zion. That He would help him in the performance of the promises and in answer to the prayers made in the sanctuary. Blessings out of the sanctuary are the sweetest blessings—tokens of God's love, the blessing of God. Strength out of Zion is spiritual strength, strength in the soul, in the inner man, and that is what we should desire for ourselves and for others in their service of the people and their sufferings.

4. That God would accept the sacrifices he has offered with his prayers, according to the law of that time, before he went out on a dangerous expedition: *"May he remember all your offerings and regard with favor your burnt sacrifices!"* (v. 3), or consume them with fire

from heaven. By this, we know that God accepts our spiritual sacrifices if by his Spirit he kindles in our souls a holy fire, and with that makes our hearts burn within us.

5. That God would crown all his enterprises and noble designs for the public welfare with the desired success (v. 4). *"May he grant you your heart's desire."* This they might pray for in faith because they knew David was a man after God's own heart and would do nothing but what was pleasing to him. Those who make it their business to glorify God can expect that God will, in one way or another, bless them. Those who walk in his counsel can promise themselves that He will fulfill theirs. *"You will decide on a matter, and it will be established for you"* (Job 22:28).

Matthew Henry

(Christianity.com, n.d.)

Daily Reflections

As you work through these reflections, allow yourself to be honest and vulnerable. If you are not sure or disagree with a comment, bring it before the Lord or discuss it with someone in your group or church. This is how we grow and learn, rather than simply brushing things aside because they do not sit well with us.

1. Why do you think it is important for us to pray for those in authority?

2. Read 1 Timothy 2:1-2. What is the benefit for us when we pray for those in power?
3. Read Colossians 1:16-17. How does this change our mindset of those in the government or those who rule over us?

5

PSALM 20 - PRAYING WITH CONFIDENCE FOR OTHERS

Now I know that the Lord saves his anointed;
he will answer him from his holy heaven
with the saving might of his right hand.
Some trust in chariots and some in horses,
but we trust in the name of the Lord our God.
They collapse and fall,
but we rise and stand upright.
O Lord, save the king!
May he answer us when we call
Psalm 20:6-9

Here is David himself triumphing in the interest he had in the prayers of good people (v. 6). It is good for any ruler and people when God pours on them a spirit of prayer. If he sees us seeking him, he will be found by us; if he causes us to hope in his word, he will establish his word to us. Now that so many who have an interest in heaven are praying for him, he doubts not but that God will hear him and grant him an answer of peace, which will:

1. come from above: God will hear him from heaven, from the throne he has prepared in heaven.
2. take its effect here below: God will hear him with the saving strength of his right hand; he will give a real answer to his prayers, and the prayers of his friends for him. He will show that he hears him by what he does for him.

David's people triumphing in God and their relation to him, and his revelation of himself to them, distinguish them from those that live without God in the world.

1. See the difference between worldly people and godly people in their confidences, (v. 7). Worldly people trust in second causes, they trust in chariots and in horses, and the more of them they can bring into the field, the more sure they are of success in their wars. "But," say the Israelites, "we neither have chariots and horses to trust, nor do we want them, but we will remember, and rely on, the name of the Lord our God, on the relation we stand to him as the Lord our God and the knowledge we have of him by his name."
2. See the difference in their confidence and by that, we are to judge the wisdom of the choice; (v. 8). Those who trusted in their chariots and horses are brought

down and fallen, and their chariots and horses were so far from saving them that they helped to sink them and made them easier prey for the conqueror (2 Sam. 8:4). But we that trust in the name of the Lord our God not only stand upright, and keep our ground, but have risen, have taken ground against the enemy, and have triumphed over them.

They conclude their prayer for the king with a Hosanna, "*O Lord, save the king!*" (v. 9). As we read this verse, it may be taken as a prayer that God would not only bless the king, "Save, Lord, give him success," but that he would make him a blessing to them, "Let the king hear us when we call to him for justice and mercy." Those that would have the goodness of their magistrates must pray for them, for they, as all other creatures, are that which God makes them be.

Or it may refer to the Messiah, that King, that King of kings; let him hear us when we call; let him come to us according to the promise, in the time appointed; let him, as the great Master of requests, receive all our petitions and present them to the Father. But many interpreters give another reading of this verse by altering the pause, Lord, save the king, and hear us when we call; and so it is a summary of the whole Psalm and is taken into our English Liturgy; O Lord! save the king, and mercifully hear us when we call on you.

In saying these verses, we should encourage ourselves to trust in God and stir up ourselves to pray earnestly, as it is our duty, for those in authority over us, that under them we may lead quiet and peaceful lives in all godliness and honesty.

Matthew Henry

(Christianity.com, n.d.)

Daily Reflections

It is one thing to pray for people and tick them off our list. But it is another to really pray for them with confidence, trusting God to hear and move on those people's behalf because of our prayers. Sometimes, our prayers lack the urgency and belief in the words that we are actually speaking.

1. Do you ever pray for the government? Not that they will do what you want them to do but that God will guide and move them?
2. What are the horses and chariots that people trust today?
3. What confidence is there for us to pray for those in positions of power or authority?

6

PSALM 36 - A PRAYER FOR MERCY AND JUSTICE

> *"Oh, continue your steadfast love to those who know you,*
> *and your righteousness to the upright of heart!*
> *Let not the foot of arrogance come upon me,*
> *nor the hand of the wicked drive me away.*
> *There the evildoers lie fallen;*
> *they are thrust down, unable to rise"*
> Psalm 36:10-12

"Continue your steadfast love to those who know you," David begins to pray. And, first, he asks in general that God would continue his mercy to all those who are godly, and then he pleads specifically on his own behalf, begging for God's help against his enemies.

Anyone who believes that it says here that God continues or extends his mercy because it is exalted above the heavens speaks foolishly. When David spoke of it in verse 5, his intention was not, as I have already said, to represent the mercy of God as shut up in heaven but simply to declare that it was spread throughout the world. What he desires is that God would continue to show, even to the end, his mercy and steadfast love toward his people.

With the steadfast love of God, he connects his righteousness, combining them as cause and effect. We have already said in another place that the righteousness of God is shown in his defense of his own people, vindicating their innocence, avenging their wrongs, restraining their enemies, and in proving himself faithful in keeping them safe and happy against all who attack them.

Now, since all this is done for them freely by God, David specifically mentions his goodness and places it first so that we may learn to depend completely on his favor. We should also notice how he describes true believers; first, he says that they know God, and secondly, that they are upright in heart. We learn from this that true godliness comes from the knowledge of God and that the light of faith must bring us to the righteousness of the heart. At the same time, we should always bear in mind that we only know God properly when we give him the honor to which he is entitled—when we place complete confidence in him.

"Let not the foot of arrogance come upon me." As I have shown before, the Psalmist speaks here of his own circumstances in the prayer. But by including all the children of God in his

prayer in the verse before, he wanted to show that he asked nothing for himself apart from others, but only desired that as one of the godly and upright, who have their eyes toward God, he might enjoy his favor. He has used the expressions, *"the foot of arrogance"* and *"the hand of the wicked"* in the same sense. As the wicked rush boldly to destroy good people, lifting up their feet to stamp on them, and having their hands ready to do wrong to them, David pleads with God to restrain their hands and their feet. He confesses that he is in danger of being exposed to their insolence, abuse, and violence unless God comes quickly to help him.

"There the evildoers lie fallen." Here he finds confidence in his prayer, not doubting that he has already received his request. And so, we see how the certainty of faith directs Christians to pray. David goes even further to confirm his confidence and hope in God, by pointing out with his finger the destruction of the wicked, even though it is still to happen in the future.

In this respect, the adverb there is not used for no purpose. While the ungodly boast of their good fortune and the world applauds them, David sees with the eye of faith, as if he was looking from a watchtower, their destruction, and he speaks about it with as much confidence as if he had already seen it happen.

For us to also attain a similar assurance, let us remember that those who would prematurely rush the time of God's vengeance on the wicked, according to their own passion and desires, make a mistake. We should leave it to the providence of God to choose the right time when, in his wisdom, he shall rise up to judgment.

When it is said, *"they are thrust down,"* the meaning is that they are agitated with doubt, and stumble as if they were in a slippery place so that in the midst of their prosperity, they have no security. Finally, it is added that they shall fall into complete destruction so that they can never be expected to rise again.

John Calvin

(CCEL, n.d.-a)

Daily Reflections

How often do we pray for God to be on our side when everything around us seems to be against us? It may be certain people against us, or the world in general, that are at odds with us, and we feel as though we may be swallowed up unless God comes through. This Psalm has all of those feelings and more—it shows confidence in God that he will triumph in the end, and so we will, too.

1. What does Calvin mean by saying that God's love and righteousness are a cause and effect?
2. Where does true godliness come from?
3. How was David able to see his enemy's downfall with such confidence, and without resentment or revenge?

7

PSALM 37 - WAITING ON GOD

*"Wait for the Lord and keep his way,
and he will exalt you to inherit the land"*
Psalm 37:34

If we want to find someone we want to meet, we ask about the places and the ways where they can be found. When waiting on God, we need to be very careful that we keep His ways; or else we never can expect to find Him.

"You meet him who joyfully works righteousness, those who remember you in your ways" (Isa. 64:5).

We can be sure that God is never and nowhere to be found but in His ways. And it is there that the soul who seeks and patiently waits will always find Him. *"Wait for the Lord and keep his way, and he will exalt you."*

See how close the connection is between the two parts of the injunction, *"Wait for the Lord"*—this has to do with worship and character—*"and keep his way"*—that deals with walk and work. The outer life must be in harmony with the inner; the inner must be the inspiration and the strength for the outer. It is God who has made His ways known in His Word for our conduct, and this gives us confidence in His grace and help in our hearts. If we do not keep His ways, our waiting on Him can bring no blessing.

The surrender to full obedience to His will is the secret of full access to all the blessings of His fellowship.

Notice how strongly this comes out in the Psalm. It speaks of the sinner who prospers in his way and calls on the believer not to worry about it. When we see people around us prosperous and happy while they forsake God's ways, and we are left in difficulty or suffering, we are in danger of worrying about what appears so strange, and then gradually yielding to seek our prosperity in their path.

The Psalm says, *"Fret not yourself... trust in the Lord, and do good... Be still before the Lord and wait patiently for him... Refrain from anger, and forsake wrath!... Turn away from evil and do good... he will not forsake his saints... The righteous shall inherit the land... The law of his God is in his heart; his steps do not slip"* (Psalm 37:1-31). And it continues in verse 34, saying the same thing for the third time: *"Wait on the Lord and keep his way."*

Do what God asks you to do; God will do more than you can ask Him to do.

And do not be afraid that you cannot keep His ways; it is this that robs you of all your confidence. It is true you do not have the strength yet to keep all His ways. But carefully keep those for which you have already received strength. Surrender yourself willingly and trustingly to keep all God's ways in the strength which will come in waiting on Him. Give up your whole being to God without reserve and without doubt; He will prove Himself God to you, and work in you that which is pleasing in His sight through Jesus Christ.

Keep His ways as you know them in the Word. Keep His ways as nature teaches them, in always doing what appears right. Keep His ways as Providence points them out. Keep His ways as the Holy Spirit suggests. Do not think of waiting on God while you say you are not willing to work in His path. However weak you feel, only be willing, and He who has worked will do so by His power.

"Wait on the Lord and keep his way." Being conscious of failure and sin might make the verse look more like a hindrance than a help in waiting on God. Do not let it be that way.

Have we not said more than once, that the starting point and groundwork of this waiting are complete and absolute weakness?

So, why not come with everything evil you feel in yourself, every memory of unwillingness, unwatchfulness, unfaithfulness, and everything that causes such self-condemnation? Put your power in God's omnipotence and you will find that waiting on God is your deliverance. Your failure has been because of one thing: You tried to conquer and obey in your own strength.

Come and bow before God until you learn that He is the God who alone is good, and alone can work any good thing. Believe that in you, and all that nature can do, there is no real power. Be content to receive from God each moment the inworking of His mighty grace and life. Then waiting on God will become the renewal of your strength to run in His ways and not be weary, to walk in His paths and never faint.

"Wait on the Lord and keep His way" will be both a command and promise.

"For God alone, O my soul, wait!" (Psalm 62:5).

Andrew Murray

(World Invisible, n.d.)

Daily Reflections

We have often heard the phrase "wait on God," and we agree with it because it is part of our Christian language and understanding. But in reality, it is a very hard thing to do. Our lives are busy, and everyone and everything demands something of us now. We have the same feeling toward God, and we cannot wait. But that is what we are told to do!

1. What is the connection between waiting on God and keeping His ways?
2. Why should failure and sin not be a hindrance to us in waiting on God?

3. Do you find it easy to wait on God or not? Why?
4. Read Isaiah 40:31. How does this encourage us to wait?

8

PSALM 119 - YOU HAVE HEARD ME

*"When I told of my ways, you answered me;
teach me your statutes!"*
Psalm 119:26

This is a beautiful description of the simplicity and sincerity of a Christian's walk with God! He spreads his whole case before God, declaring his ways of sinfulness, difficulty, and conduct. It is our privilege to let our Father know all our cares and needs so that we may be pitied by His love, guided by His counsel, and confirmed by His strength. Who would not find relief by unburdening himself to his Father? This showing of ourselves to God—declaring our ways of sin before Him without deceit—is the short and sure way of rest.

"You heard me." *"For when I kept silent, my bones wasted away through my groaning all day long"* (Psalm 32:3). When the voice of confession was silent, cries and sorrow were disregarded. It was not the voice of the penitent child. But now, as soon as words of confession are on his lips, or on the first motivation of contrition in his heart; the full and free pardon, which had been signed in heaven, comes down with royal parental love to his soul. *"I said, 'I will confess my transgressions to the LORD,' and you forgave the iniquity of my sin"* (Psalm 32:5).

What parental tenderness with which *"transgression is forgiven, whose sin is covered"* (Psalm 32:1). And yet, how necessary to the free declaration of our ways is an acquaintance with the way of forgiveness! If our High Priest had not gone up to heaven, how terrible it would be to know that everything was *"naked and exposed to the eyes of him to whom we must give account"* (Heb. 4:13). Then we could only have covered our transgressions like Adam, by *"by hiding my iniquity in my heart"* (Job 31:33). But now, even though our ways are so wicked and crooked that we hate ourselves because of them, we are still encouraged to boldly declare them all before God, with the confidence of finding acceptance and grace.

Having this sincere and child-like spirit, then we find the obligation of walking worthy of this mercy. That is why we need to pray for continual teaching. The same heavenly guidance that brought us this far, we need for every successive step to the end: *Teach me your way, O LORD, that I may walk in your truth"* (Psalm 86:11). *"I have declared my"* ignorance, sinfulness, and my whole experience before You, looking for Your forgiving mercy, Your teaching Spirit, and assisting grace, *"and You heard me."* Continue to teach me more of Yourself!

The hypocrite can pray like this, but he never opens his heart and declares his ways before God. Are we sincere in our dealings with Him? How often do we treat the Almighty as if we were tired of dealing with Him? And even when we do declare our ways before Him, are we not content to leave the result unfinished? We do not watch for the answer to our prayer. It will come in the diligent exercise of faith, but not in our way.

We may have asked for physical blessings, and we receive spiritual ones. We may have asked for deliverance from a trial, and we receive the grace that is sufficient to bear it. But this is the Lord's wise and gracious answer—*"You heard me."* How amazing are those blessings that have been received by prayer! They are such encouragement to pray again. It is not our inevitable weakness, nor our lamented dullness, nor our abhorred wanderings, nor our opposed distractions, nor our mistaken unbelief that can shut out prayer. If iniquity is not hidden in our hearts, then we can always hear our Savior's voice: *Truly, truly, I say to you, whatever you ask of the Father in my name, he will give it to you. Until now you have asked nothing in my name. Ask, and you will receive, that your joy may be full"* (John 16:23-24).

Charles Bridges

(Grace Gems, n.d.-a)

Daily Reflections

This is a crucial part of prayer—believing and knowing that God hears us. Most times, it feels as though he is not there, or that our cries for help do not go further than the ceiling. But this Psalm declares it as truth, as a fact! With that kind of confidence, our prayers change because we are sure that He has heard.

1. It speaks here of a "child-like spirit." Do you have this? Why or why not?
2. What is the difference between a child-like belief and a hypocrite?
3. When you get something other than what you prayed for, what is your response? What should our response be according to this passage?

9

PSALM 112 - A FIRM HEART TO PRAY

*"He is not afraid of bad news;
his heart is firm, trusting in the Lord"*
Psalm 112:7

Not Afraid

I begin with the righteous man's privilege. *"He is not afraid of bad news."* When there are rumors of evil approaching, the godly man shall not be disturbed by it in his mind. He shall not panic or fear.

First, not that the righteous man is unaware of danger, or how else could he humble himself under God's mighty hand?

Second, not that some clouds of fear won't come into his mind. Though grace subdues our instinct, it does not expel instinct. But the meaning of the verse is this, *"He is not afraid of bad news."* A righteous man shall not be afraid with a distracting fear. Such a fear takes him away from his duty of prayer and worship and makes him useless for God's service.

"*He is not afraid of bad news*" with a fainting fear so that his heart dies within him. It was like this with Saul: *"Then Saul fell at once full length on the ground, filled with fear"* (1 Samuel 28:20). He fainted in his fear.

Trusting

In the next words, we see the foundation or reason why a godly person will not be afraid or amazed at evil news. *"His heart is firm, trusting in the Lord."* There is the ground. This makes him like the leviathan, without fear; *"His heart is firm, trusting in the Lord."*

Fixing the heart shows stability and assurance of spirit. An unfixed heart is just like a ship without stabilizing counterweight, blown up and down in the water. *"He alone is my rock and my salvation, my fortress; I shall not be greatly shaken"* (Psalm 62:2).

Fixing the heart is for holy duties. The person whose heart is firm on God serves God with joy, with cheerfulness. An unfixed heart is a heart that is not fit for duty. A shaking hand is not suitable to write. An unfixed heart is unfit to pray or meditate; it runs after other pleasures. Surely, then, a firm attitude of heart is an excellent attitude of the heart. You know that when the milk is settled, it turns to cream. So, when the heart is settled and fixed on God, it is in the best setting.

Trusting in God fixes the heart. The heart is firm, trusting in the Lord—it is fixed by trusting. Faith frees the heart from those commotions which cause trembling and shaking. It fixes the heart on God. As a star is fixed in the sky, so a believer's soul is fixed on God. Faith makes the heart turn to God as a needle turns to a magnet. Faith fixes the heart.

Oh! Let us strive for this heart-fixing grace of faith above all else. Trusting in God supports, gives life, and holds up the heart in death-threatening dangers. Oh, get this heart-fixing grace of faith!

Oh! Let us strive for this true faith and trust, to have our hearts fixed on God in evil times. Faith is the heart-establishing and heart-strengthening grace. *"His heart is established, he shall not be afraid"* (Psalm 112:8 KJV). The Hebrew word for establish means "the heart is shored up" and "the heart is underpinned." It is a metaphor that speaks about a house that is underpinned or supported by strong material. So, faith shores up and strengthens the heart when it is about to sink. Oh! Get this heart-fixing grace of faith. Then you will be resolved and undaunted even in the worst of times and dangers.

To encourage your faith, remember these two things, you who strive and persevere for the church's deliverance: Faith and prayer are the two midwives that deliver God's Church when she is in suffering. *"Help us, O Lord our God"*—there was the prayer; *"for we rely on you"*—there was the faith (2 Chron. 14:11). When we build our reliance and confidence on God, He is obliged by his own honor to defend and save us. *"In him my heart trusts, and I am helped"* (Psalm 28:7).

To sum up everything, let us strive to have our hearts fixed on God by holy trust above everything else. Trust His heart—where you cannot trace His hand! Trust God for protection in this life, and salvation in the next life.

Trusting in God is a cure for all diseases. Faith is the universal cure! Does the orphan trust himself in the hands of his guardian? Does the patient trust his life in the hands of the doctor? Should we not trust our souls in God's hand? *"He is a shield for all those who take refuge in him"* (2 Samuel 22:31). If we want to master our fears and worries, we must give up human reasoning and grow our faith. Then you will not be afraid of bad news, for the heart will be firm, trusting in the Lord.

Thomas Watson

(Grace Gems, n.d.)

Daily Reflections

It is good to work through these readings and reflections with a notebook. Make notes as you go along—thoughts, questions, revelations—these are important to allow your mind to be open to God teaching you. If you are not sure, write it down. In time, God will show you.

1. Are you someone who is afraid of bad news? Why?
2. What makes it possible to not fear bad news?
3. How do we get a "fixed heart"?
4. What is the special connection between faith and prayer that is shown in this passage?

10

PSALM 23 - WHO CAN HEAR HIS VOICE?

"The Lord is my shepherd;
I shall not want"
Psalm 23:1

The foundation thought of this part of the Psalm, as well as the next, is found in the opening words, "Jehovah is my Shepherd." The example of the shepherd is one of frequent occurrence in the Bible. It was a favorite illustration used by Jesus. It stands for love and care and protection and provision on God's part, and for trust and obedience and following on our part (John 10:1, 18, 26-29; Matt. 9:36).

To pray the words "Jehovah is my Shepherd" is to say that He loves me with the tenderest love. How an eastern shepherd loves his sheep is brought out in Luke 15:4-6. How the Lord loves His sheep is brought out in John 10:11, *"I am the good shepherd. The good shepherd lays down his life for the sheep,"* and in John 10:3-4, *"To him the gatekeeper opens. The sheep hear his voice, and he calls his own sheep by name and leads them out. When he has brought out all his own, he goes before them, and the sheep follow him, for they know his voice."* Because "Jehovah is my Shepherd," He loves me, He will secure my safety and my welfare even if it takes the sacrifice of Himself, as it did.

To say "Jehovah is my Shepherd" is to say that I am the subject of His ever-watchful and tender care. Since "Jehovah is my Shepherd," He will protect me and, therefore, I need not fear the lion, the bear, the wolf, or the devil and all his hosts because my Shepherd is always near and is ever mighty and will deliver me out of their mouth. All I need to see is that I am one of His sheep, and therefore can rightly say, "Jehovah is my Shepherd."

To pray the words "Jehovah is my Shepherd" is also to say, Jehovah will provide for me, that he will find me good and sufficient pastures. It is a shepherd's business to feed the sheep and the lambs, and by making Himself my Shepherd, Jehovah has undertaken to make it His business to provide me pasture and He will do it; so no wonder the Psalmist continues, "I shall not want."

Who has a right to say "Jehovah is my Shepherd"? Everybody? Most assuredly not. There are certain well-defined and clearly stated conditions of being one of Jehovah's sheep, and only those who meet the conditions have the right to pray,

"Jehovah is my Shepherd." But everyone can meet the conditions.

The Conditions

We can find these conditions in John 10:3-5, 27: *"To him the gatekeeper opens. The sheep hear his voice, and he calls his own sheep by name and leads them out. When he has brought out all his own, he goes before them, and the sheep follow him, for they know his voice. A stranger they will not follow, but they will flee from him, for they do not know the voice of strangers... My sheep hear my voice, and I know them, and they follow me."* We see here that the conditions of being Jehovah's sheep are, first, that we hear His voice—that we listen and attend to what Jehovah has to say. The man who is neglecting the voice of Jehovah as it speaks in the Bible and through His Spirit, and the man who refuses to attend to that voice, has no right to repeat the 23rd Psalm and pray, "Jehovah is my Shepherd."

Second, that we follow Him. The one who is not following the Lord has no right to pray the words, "Jehovah is my Shepherd." Third, that we do not listen to the voice of strangers, but flee from them. The man or woman who is willing to go after and listen to every new gospel spinner that comes along has no right to pray, "Jehovah is my Shepherd." The Lord's sheep will not follow a stranger but flee from him.

Two people were once looking over the Bible together as the 23rd Psalm was read. One took out a pencil and drew a mark under the third word, 'my.' At the close of the service, the other said, "Why did you draw that line under 'my?'" The other replied, "The Lord is MY Shepherd, and I wondered if He were yours."

R. A. Torrey

(Torrey, 1915)

Daily Reflections

One of the most well-known and beloved of all Psalms is opened up for us here. Even if it is just the introductory verse, it still sets the stage for the rest of the Psalm as we read it. But in the context of prayer, it is revealing in its simplicity in being able to address God in this way and call Him our shepherd.

1. Do you ever see God as your shepherd? Why?
2. Do you ever see yourself as a sheep?
3. What is meant by the phrase *"for they know his voice"*?
4. What are the conditions for being able to call God our shepherd?

11

PSALM 10 - DAVID PLEADS HIS CASE

"Arise, O Lord; O God, lift up your hand;
forget not the afflicted"
Psalm 10:12

David pleads to encourage his own faith in these petitions:

1. He pleads the insults which these oppressors have put on God: "Lord, it is for Your own cause that we beg You to appear; the enemies have done this, and so, for Your glory do not let them go unpunished" (v. 13): *"Why do the wicked renounce God and say in his heart, 'You will not call to account'?"*

The Psalmist is surprised at the wickedness of the wicked. It upsets good men to think of the contempt thrown on God by the sin of sinners, on his laws, promises, favors, and judgments; all are despised and made fun of. Why do the wicked renounce God? It is because they do not know him. He is always surprised at the patience of God toward them. It is because the day of judgment is still to come when the measure of their iniquity is full.

1. He pleads how much notice God took of the disrespect and iniquity of these oppressors (v. 14): "Do they think that You will never see it? Let them know that You have seen it, it is all known to You and observed by You. Not only have You seen it, but You will repay it by Your just and avenging hand."
2. He pleads the dependence which the oppressed had on Him: *"To you the helpless commits himself; you have been the helper of the fatherless"* (v. 13).
3. He pleads God's relationship with us as a great God. *"The Lord is king forever and ever"* (v. 16). It is the duty of a king to administer justice to evil-doers and protection of those that do well. To whom should the injured subjects appeal but to the sovereign?
4. He pleads how God had heard and answered their prayers before (v. 17): "Lord, many times You have heard our desires and never said to us, 'Seek in vain.' Why can we not hope for more of the miracles, the blessings, which we heard about?"
5. He pleads their expectations of God: *"The Lord has heard my plea; the Lord accepts my prayer"* (Psalm 6:9). But see how God hears prayer. He first prepares the

heart of his people and then gives them an answer of peace. He prepares the heart for prayer by motivating holy desires, strengthening our faith, fixing the thoughts, and raising the emotions, and then he graciously accepts the prayer. He prepares the heart for the blessing that is prayed for, makes us ready to receive it and use it well, and then gives it to us. The preparation of the heart is from the Lord, and we must seek Him for it.

See what He will do in answer to prayer. He will *"do justice to the fatherless and the oppressed"* (v. 18). He will put an end to the fury of the persecutors. They will come this far, but no further. See how little the Psalmist now thinks of that proud persecutor whom he had been describing in this Psalm, and how he hardly speaks of him now that he had been considering God's sovereignty. He is just a man. Why should we be afraid of the fury of the oppressor when he is just a man that will die, a son of man that shall be as grass? (Isa. 51:12). He that protects us is the Lord of heaven. God has the oppressor in a chain, and can easily restrain him so that he cannot do what he wants. When God speaks the word, Satan will not deceive anymore (Rev. 20:3); he will not oppress any longer.

Matthew Henry

(Christianity.com, n.d.)

Daily Reflections

Pleading often sounds degrading, as if we have to beg God for everything. However, if we think of a courtroom where pleading your case before a judge is not groveling in the dirt, but stating your situation and the reasons why you should be heard and answered, then our idea of what David is doing in this Psalm changes.

1. Do you ever use God's own words or attributes as reasons why He should answer you?
2. Why do you think this type of praying encourages our faith, as it did for David?
3. If you look at the six pleas outlined here, which one do you identify with the most? Why?

12

PSALM 123 - LIFTING UP OUR EYES

"To you I lift up my eyes,
O you who are enthroned in the heavens!
Behold, as the eyes of servants
look to the hand of their master,
as the eyes of a maidservant
to the hand of her mistress,
so our eyes look to the Lord our God,
till he has mercy upon us"
Psalm 123:1-2

We are climbing. The first step (Psalm 120) saw us crying about our troublesome surroundings, and the next saw us lifting our eyes to the hills and resting in assured security; from this, we rose to delight in the house of the Lord. But here we look to the Lord himself, and this is the highest ascent of all. The eyes are now looking above the hills, and above Jehovah's footstool on earth, to his throne in the heavens.

"To you I lift up my eyes." It is good to have someone to look up to. The Psalmist looked so high that he could look no higher—not to the hills, but to the God of the hills. He believed in a personal God and knew nothing of that modern pantheism which is nothing more than atheism wearing a fig leaf. The uplifted eyes naturally and instinctively represent the state of heart that fixes desire, hope, confidence, and expectation on the Lord. God is everywhere, and yet it is most natural to think of him as being above us.

"O you who are enthroned in the heavens!" If we have a thousand helpers, our eyes should still be toward the Lord. The higher the Lord is, the better for our faith, since that height represents power, glory, and excellence, and these will be all engaged on our behalf.

We should be very thankful for spiritual eyes; the blind men of this world, however much human learning they may possess, cannot see God, for in heavenly matters they are blind. Yet we must use our eyes with a resolution, for they will not go up to the Lord by themselves, but they tend to look down, in, or anywhere but to him. It is a blessed condescension on God's part that he allows us to lift up our eyes to his glorious high throne. Even more, he invites and even commands us to do so. When we are looking to the Lord in hope, it is good to tell him so in prayer. The Psalmist uses his voice as well as his eye.

It is helpful to the heart to use the tongue, and we do well to address ourselves in words and sentences to the God who hears his people. Let us not think that certain times of the day are not good for waiting on the Lord; no hour of the night is too dark for us to look to him.

"Behold"—See, O Lord, how we look to you, and in your mercy look on us.

"As the eyes of servants look to the hand of their master." The servant must keep his eyes on his master, or he might miss an instruction and fail to obey it. So, the sanctified man lifts his eyes to God and tries to learn the divine will from every one of the signs that the Lord uses. Creation, providence, grace—these are all from Jehovah's hand, and from each of them a part of our duty is to be learned; therefore, we should carefully study them to discover his will.

"So our eyes look to the Lord our God." True Christians, like obedient servants, look to the Lord their God in reverence. They have holy awe and inner fear of the great and glorious One. They watch, obediently doing his commandments, guided by his eye. Their constant gaze is fixed attentively on all that comes from the Most High. They look continuously because there never is a time when they are off duty. On the Lord they fix their eyes expectantly, looking for supply, support, and safety from his hands, waiting that he may have mercy on them. Only to him they look, they have no other confidence; and they learn to look submissively, waiting patiently for the Lord, seeking both in activity and suffering to glorify his name.

Are we trained to serve like this? Though we are sons and daughters, have we learned the full obedience of servants? Have we surrendered self, and bowed our will before the heavenly Majesty? Do we desire in all things to be at the Lord's disposal? If so, then we are happy. Though we are made joint heirs with Christ—yet for now we are servants, and should look at them for our example.

"Till he has mercy upon us." God has his time and season, and we must wait until it comes. For the trial of our faith, our Lord may wait for a while, but in the end, the vision will be fulfilled. Mercy is what we need, what we look for, and what our Lord will show us. Even those who look to the Lord, with that holy look described here, still need mercy, and as they cannot claim it by right, they wait for it until sovereign grace chooses to grant it. Blessed are those servants whom their Master shall find so doing.

Waiting on the Lord is a position suitable both for earth and Heaven. It is the right and fitting condition for a servant of the Lord. It is a great mercy to be enabled to wait for mercy. God, when he sees us placing an exclusive dependence on his protection, and renouncing all confidence in our own resources, will, as our defender, come and shield us from all the harm.

Charles Spurgeon

(Grace Gems, 2022)

Daily Reflections

Spurgeon has such a wonderful style of writing that it brings us to a place where we are both encouraged and challenged at the same time. By outlining and breaking down this Psalm for us, verse by verse, he makes it accessible for us to understand where we are.

1. Are you able to "lift up your eyes" and see God as you pray to Him?
2. How does the way we look to God change when we see ourselves as servants waiting for His command or His generosity?
3. Why do you think waiting on the Lord is so difficult for us to do?

13

PSALM 123 - HAVE MERCY ON US

*"Have mercy upon us, O Lord, have mercy upon us,
for we have had more than enough of contempt.
Our soul has had more than enough
of the scorn of those who are at ease,
of the contempt of the proud"*
Psalm 123:3-4

"Have mercy upon us, O Lord, have mercy upon us." He hangs on the word 'mercy' and uses it in passionate prayer. It is good for us to pray about everything, and turn everything into prayer; especially when we are reminded of a great necessity, we should catch at it as a keynote, and pitch our tune to it.

The repetition of the prayer here is meant to express the eagerness of the Psalmist's spirit and his urgent need: What he needed quickly, he begs for persistently.

Note that he is speaking in the plural—all Christians need mercy; they all seek it; they will all have it, therefore we pray, *"Have mercy upon us."* A servant, when corrected, looks to his master's hand for the punishment to stop, and we look to the Lord for mercy and beg for it with all our hearts. Our opponents will have no mercy on us. Let us not ask for it from their hands, but turn to the God of mercy, and seek only his help.

"For we have had more than enough of contempt," and this is an acid that eats into the soul. Observe the emphatic words. Contempt is bitterness, a nasty pill mixed with bile—whoever feels it will find it good to cry for mercy to God. Filled with contempt, as if the bitter wine had been poured in until it was up to the brim. This had become the main thought of their minds, the strange sorrow of their hearts. Excluding all other feelings, a sense of scorn monopolized the soul and made it unspeakably terrible.

Another word is used as an adverb in other translations—*"exceedingly filled"* (Psalm 123:4 KJV). Filled even to running over, as if it was pressed down and then heaped up. A little contempt they could bear, but now they were satiated with it, and tired of it. Do we wonder about the repetition of the word *'mercy'* three times? Nothing is more wounding, embittering, festering than disdain and scorn. When our companions think little of us, we are far too quick to think little of ourselves and the consolations prepared for us. But, to be filled with communion with Jesus, then contempt will run off from us, and never be able to fill us with its biting vinegar.

"Our soul has had more than enough of the scorn of those who are at ease." Knowing no troubles of their own, the easy ones grow cruel and mock the people of the Lord. Already secretly hating Christians, they do not show it by openly scorning them.

Note those who do this: They are not the poor, humble, or troubled, but those who have a great life and are self-content. They are in easy circumstances; they are easy in the heart because their conscience is dead, and so they easily mock holiness. They need nothing and have no heavy work demanded from them. They are at ease and not worried about improving because their conceit of themselves is boundless. Such people take things easily, and therefore, they scorn the holy carefulness of those who watch the hand of the Lord. They say: "Who is the Lord that we should obey his voice?" Then they turn round with a contemptuous look and sneer at those who fear the Lord. They must be careful, as their contempt for the godly will quickly increase their misery.

Put someone perfectly at ease and they will mock the righteous who are suffering, and they become proud in their heart and conduct.

"Of the contempt of the proud." The proud think so much of themselves that they think less of those who are better than themselves. Pride is both contemptible and contemptuous. To become the target of contempt is quite another matter. Great hearts have been broken and brave spirits have been

crushed beneath the terrible power of lies, and the horrible disease of contempt.

For our comfort, we can remember that our Lord was also despised and rejected by men—yet he did not stop from his perfect service until he was exalted to live in the heavens. Let us bear our share of this evil which still rages under the sun, and let us firmly believe that the contempt of the ungodly shall turn to our honor in the world to come. Even now, it serves as a certificate that we are not of the world, for if we were of the world, the world would love us as its own.

Charles Spurgeon

(Grace Gems, 2022)

Daily Reflections

The Psalms are filled with prayers and songs asking for God's mercy. It is a vital part of Christianity to understand that we should not just take it for granted, but we should ask for it, plead for it, daily. Although God gives it to us freely, He also wants us to see how much we need it by asking for it.

1. What is meant by God's mercy? Read James 2:13 and 2 Peter 3:9.
2. Why does Spurgeon make such a big thing about *"exceedingly filled"*?
3. What should be our comfort in times when we are mocked and despised?

14

PSALM 27 - ONE THING I ASKED FOR

"One thing have I asked of the Lord,
that will I seek after:
that I may dwell in the house of the Lord
all the days of my life,
to gaze upon the beauty of the Lord
and to inquire in his temple"
Psalm 27:4

Let us desire God to reveal himself in his laws to us more and more, and desire him to give us spiritual eyes more and more to see him. Sometimes he hides himself in his commands so that we cannot see the beauty of things. Let us, therefore, desire him to reveal himself, to take away that veil that is between us and holy things, and between us and grace, and comfort, that he would take away that spiritual veil, and reveal himself to us, and shine on us in Christ, that he would manifest his love to us, and give us spiritual eyes to see him.

Prayer is an excellent way to start, and when we are busy doing Christian things, let us lift up our hearts to God to reveal his truths to us.

Praying for Clarity

There are many veils between us and holy things. Let us desire God to take them all away—of error, ignorance, and unbelief—and to shine so clearly to us by his Spirit, that we may see him more clearly. Now, a man may more clearly see and feel God at peace with him by the Spirit, and clearly see and feel the comfort of forgiveness of sins, and of any promise that is unfolded; and it has a marvelous influence on the emotions, to comfort and to breed peace and joy. And that is one sign that we profit by the commands of God; when our daily prayers work peace and comfort, and spiritual strength against temptations and corruptions. Therefore, we are to pray to God that his Holy Spirit would reveal his secrets to us, and with revelation influence our souls, that there may be grace and comfort through the ordinances to our souls. Prayer must accompany the Christian practices and rituals; because the ordinance itself is an empty thing unless the Spirit accompanies it.

Seeking Spiritual Things

Let us know what our souls were made for—to dwell in the meditation of the beauty of God. They are for union and communion with God in his ordinances, to grow in nearer communion with God by his Spirit, to have more knowledge, more love and joy, and delight in the best things daily. Our souls are for these things that will make us gracious here, and glorious forever after in heaven. It is a great disorder when we study and care only for earthly things.

The things of God's Spirit are holy and excellent when there is such a taste and desire in the soul for them. *"My sheep hear my voice"* (John 10:27), says Jesus. *"Like newborn infants, long for the pure spiritual milk, that by it you may grow up into salvation"* (1 Pet. 2:2). A person can know he is a true child of the church if he desires the sincere milk of the word, to grow better and more holy. If he delights in the voice of God in the ministry and is motivated to the truth and ordinances of God, it is the character of a good Christian.

David comforted himself with this: *"Oh how I love your law! It is my meditation all the day"* (Psalm 119:97). Oh! that we could say the same thing, that we could delight in this beauty of God, as David says here: *"One thing have I asked of the Lord, that will I seek after: that I may dwell in the house of the Lord all the days of my life, to gaze upon the beauty of the Lord and to inquire in his temple."*

Richard Sibbes

(The Highway, n.d.)

Daily Reflections

It is good to have your Bible close by as you read through these passages and work through the reflections. Reading the verses in context, seeing different translations and their meanings, finding references to other portions of scripture, and being reminded of verses that you already know are all ways of studying the Bible and understanding it more.

1. Why do you think God hides Himself or hides certain things from us?
2. What is the role of the Holy Spirit when it comes to these situations?
3. What is meant by *"pure spiritual milk"*?
4. Do you desire these things from God and ask Him to reveal more to you?

15

PSALM 122 - PRAY FOR THE CHURCH

"Pray for the peace of Jerusalem!
'May they be secure who love you!
Peace be within your walls
and security within your towers!'
For my brothers and companions' sake
I will say, 'Peace be within you!'
For the sake of the house of the Lord our God,
I will seek your good"
Psalm 122:6-9

In this Psalm, David congratulates himself and the whole church on the fact that a place had been appointed for the ark of the covenant, and that God had chosen a place where his name should always be called on. Afterward, to motivate and encourage the faithful to engage in the worship of the sanctuary, he briefly declares that the prosperous condition of the people depended on God's having chosen the seat of royalty to be at Jerusalem, from where he could defend, maintain, and assist his people

David encourages all Christians to pray for the prosperity of the holy city. To encourage them in this, he promises that they will be blessed if they do so. The reason why he was so concerned about the prosperity of Jerusalem was because the welfare of the whole church was connected with that kingdom and priesthood.

Now, if the church was destroyed, we would suffer along with it, so it is not surprising to find David recommending all believers to cultivate this concern about the church. If we want to pray correctly, let us always begin with pleading that the Lord would preserve this sacred community. Whoever is concerned only about their own personal advantages is indifferent to the common good, and they show a lack of godliness. Their selfish desires for their own prosperity will profit nothing in their prayers, since they do not observe the command. The promise which is added immediately after confirms this: *"May they be secure who love you!"*

Although the Hebrew verb שלה, shalah, signifies to live in quietness or peace, yet as the Hebrew noun for peace, from which it is derived, is used for a joyful and happy condition, he announces to all the godly who have the well-being of the church in their heart, that they shall enjoy the blessing of God and prosperous life. This sentence frequently occurs in the Prophecies of Isaiah, from the 54th chapter to the end of the book.

"Peace be within your walls and security within your towers!" The term peace signifies nothing else than prosperity. The noun שלוה, shalvah, in the second clause sometimes signifies rest, but it is more frequently taken for abundance or prosperity. David prays for the prosperity of the church throughout its whole extent. When he offers supplication for its external prosperity, he was not unconcerned about its internal state or spiritual well-being, but using the comparison of walls, he wishes that on all sides the blessing of God may secure and fortify the holy city.

The unity among the citizens of a city is compared to buildings, compacted together by skillful and elegant workmanship so that there is nothing imperfect, but a beautiful harmony. By this, David teaches us that the church can only remain in a state of safety when there is a sense of togetherness in her, and when, being joined together by faith and love, she cultivates a holy unity.

David is not influenced by personal considerations but by a concern for the whole church, which he embraced with his heart. Those who are indifferent to its condition are cruel and ungodly because it is *"a pillar and buttress of the truth"* (1 Tim. 3:15). If the body is destroyed, how can each of the members avoid also being destroyed? The church is not an empty title but must be sought for where the true faith continues.

"For the sake of the house of the Lord our God, I will seek your good." In this verse, he adds a second reason why he cared for the Church—because the worship of God would go to ruin unless Jerusalem continued standing. If religion is a matter

of heart-work, we should take an interest in the prosperity of the church.

John Calvin

(CCEL, n.d.-a)

Daily Reflections

Many times we find ourselves praying for our own situations and our families. This is normal since we are surrounded by immediate needs almost every day. But in this Psalm, we see the importance of the role the church plays in our spiritual lives, and how vital it is that we pray for its well-being and security.

1. Do you ever pray for your church locally? And the church globally?
2. Calvin sees that praying for Jerusalem is not necessarily for a physical city. What is he suggesting?
3. Why are unity, harmony, and peace so important in the church?

16

PSALM 46 - BE STILL

"Be still, and know that I am God.
I will be exalted among the nations,
I will be exalted in the earth!"
Psalm 46:10

This Psalm is a prayer and song of the church in a time of great wars in the world. Therefore, the church sees God as her refuge, strength, and present help in times of the greatest troubles. *"God is our refuge and strength, a very present help in trouble. Therefore we will not fear though the earth gives way, though the mountains be moved into the heart of the sea, though its waters roar and foam, though the mountains tremble at its swelling"* (v. 1-3). The church boasts of God, not only as being her help, by defending her from the desolations and calamities that the rest of the world was involved in, but also by supplying her with refreshment, comfort, and joy in those times by a never-ending river. *There is a river whose streams make glad the city of God, the holy habitation of the Most High. God is in the midst of her; she shall not be moved; God will help her when morning dawn"* (v. 4-5).

In the 6th and 8th verses we are told about the terrible changes and disasters which were in the world: *The nations rage, the kingdoms totter; he utters his voice, the earth melts. Come, behold the works of the Lord, how he has brought desolations on the earth"* (v. 6, 8). In the next verse, we see elegantly described the manner in which God delivers the church from these catastrophes, and especially from the destruction of war and the rage of their enemies: *He makes wars cease to the end of the earth; he breaks the bow and shatters the spear; he burns the chariots with fire"* (v. 9). He stops the wars when they are against his people; he breaks the weapons that are aimed at his believers.

Then we find the words of our key verse: *"Be still, and know that I am God."* The great works of God, those that showed his sovereignty, had been described in the previous verses. In the awful destruction that he caused, and by delivering his people from terrible things, he showed his greatness and dominion. This is how he manifested his power and sovereignty, and so commands all to be still and to know that he is God. Why? Because he says, *"I will be exalted among the nations, I will be exalted in the earth!"*

In these words we can see:

1. There is a duty to be still before God and in his provision. This implies that we must be still in our words—not speaking against his supply of provision, or complaining about it; not complaining with words things we know nothing about, or justifying ourselves, and speaking great eloquent words of vanity. We must be still in our actions and outward behavior, so as not to oppose God in what he does; and as to the inner attitude of our hearts, cultivating a calm and quiet submission of the soul to the sovereign pleasure of God, whatever it be.
2. We can observe this duty regarding the divinity of God. His being God is a sufficient reason why we should be still before him, in no wise complaining, objecting, or opposing, but calmly and humbly submitting to him.
3. How we must fulfill this duty of being still before God—in that we know him to be God. Our submission is to be such as is fitting for created beings with logic and understanding. God does not require us to submit without reason but to submit as seeing the reason and ground of submission—the simple consideration that God is God should be sufficient to stop all objections and opposition against the divine sovereign dispensations.

Jonathan Edwards

(Monergism, n.d.)

Daily Reflections

These words have been quoted and used so many times that they sometimes lose their significance. In fact, reading the whole Psalm will paint a very different context than what we might use the verse for. Edwards makes some interesting points that challenge our notion of this.

1. Read the whole of Psalm 46. What is the context or setting of it?
2. Why are the words, *"I will be exalted among the nations, I will be exalted in the earth!"* so important in following our key verse?
3. What are the three ways that we are called to be still?

17

PSALM 40 - GOD ANSWERS IN TRIALS

> *"I waited patiently for the Lord;*
> *he inclined to me and heard my cry.*
> *He drew me up from the pit of destruction,*
> *out of the miry bog,*
> *and set my feet upon a rock,*
> *making my steps secure"*
> Psalm 40:1-2

"*I waited patiently for the Lord.*" Jesus is an example to the church, and here we see the result of waiting patiently. "*He inclined unto me and heard my cry.*" If we patiently wait for the Lord, the result will be that the answer will come according to our desire. We should keep this in mind so that we may receive the blessing for which we have asked God.

Nothing is obtained by impatience, we only dishonor God by it.

Verse 2 refers to the sufferings of Jesus as our substitute. When He passed through the hour of darkness, this was fulfilled. *"The pit of destruction"* shows us how terrible the hour He had to go through was. But this did not continue forever. He was brought out of it. And even though we do not have to suffer as a substitute for others, we might also be found in the horrible pit and the miry clay to a certain extent. But it will not last forever—we will also have our feet put on a rock.

Jesus passed through suffering once and for all, and His feet were set on a rock, and His way was established. But ever since His resurrection, this work has been further and further developed, and will be developed further and further until His return (Psalm 36:8).

"Many will see and fear, and put their trust in the Lord" (v. 3). This second part of the verse we see is always being fulfilled; millions have been brought to believe in Jesus, and millions will still come to be brought to a knowledge of Him. Comparatively, the number may seem small to us, but it will be seen how innumerable it is in the end!

"Blessed is the man who makes the Lord his trust" (v. 4). This is a real blessing, to make Jesus our trust for the salvation of our souls so that we can obtain all we really need while passing through this time of tears in trial and difficulty. The only remedy is to trust in the Lord, and only then will we be really blessed and happy. The word 'blessed' is the same in the

original as 'happy,' so we can read it as "Happy is that man who makes the Lord his trust."

We should remember the next verse for our comfort when we are in trial, in difficulty, in affliction—*"You have multiplied, O Lord my God, your wondrous deeds"* (v. 5). Then comes a remarkable sentence: *"And your thoughts toward us."* Here Jesus is in union with the church, to us. Not "to me" but to *"us,"* in intimate union with the church, for we are members of that body where Jesus is Head. His mind is toward us, He is thinking about us! He never loses sight of us, never forgets us. And then how many they are we read in what follows: *"I will proclaim and tell of them, yet they are more than can be told"* (v. 5). God thinks of us so often that the thoughts which He has toward us, regarding us, these thoughts are so many they cannot be counted.

Who is He thinking about? About poor sinners who deserve nothing but hell? We should say to ourselves, "He is thinking about me, wicked, guilty sinner, deserving nothing but hell, yet I am dear to the heart of God, so precious in His sight, that He is looking on me as He looks on His only Son because I am one with Him. I am a member of that body of which He is the Head. I am united to Him, and therefore He is always thinking about me."

"In sacrifice and offering you have not delighted" (v. 6). Originally, this was the law —it was instituted because of man's weakness, otherwise it would not have been. *"But you have given me an open ear."* When a slave was set free and chose to remain a slave, then he was to be brought to the door, and his ear was pierced, and he had to remain the bondservant of his master

forever. Now, Jesus makes Himself the bondservant of God. In perfect obedience to God at all times and under all circumstances, Jesus secured a righteousness which, through faith in His name, we stand as justified ones before God. So He did not just fulfill the law in our place but bore the penalty of the law.

George Muller

(Mullers, n.d.)

Daily Reflections

Trials and hardships are a big part of human life, so it is no surprise that we find so many in Psalms. As a reflection of the honesty and reality we go through, these prayers and songs reveal how we can and should approach God in prayer.

1. Do you find it easy to wait patiently for the Lord? Why is it so hard sometimes?
2. Muller sees this as a continual work, as being developed further and further. Do you agree with this?
3. The picture of a pierced ear and a bondservant are very clear and visual. Why is Jesus bearing our penalty such a key part of our Christianity?

18

PSALM 119 - A PRAYER FOR COMFORT

*"Let your steadfast love comfort me
according to your promise to your servant"*
Psalm 119:76

Several of the verses before speak of hardship. The Psalmist now prays for alleviation from this. But of what kind? He does not plead *"with the Lord about this, that it should leave me"* (2 Cor. 12:8). No. His repeated acknowledgments of the support during this time, and the benefits he gained from it, had reconciled him to continue with the Lord. All that he needs, and all that he asks for, is God's merciful kindness on his soul. So, he submits to His justice in many trials, and expects consolation under them, solely on the ground of His free favor.

It is hard to hold on under a long trial without this precious support. Patience can stop us from grumbling but only a sense of love keeps us from fainting. Holiness is our service—affliction is our exercise—comfort is our gracious reward. All the candles in the world, without the sun, can never make the day. The whole earth in its brightest imaginations, without the Lord's love, can never uplift or revive the soul. It does not matter where we are or what we have. Unless the Lord meets us and blesses us with His merciful kindness for our comfort, it is *"a dry and weary land where there is no water"* (Psalm 63:1).

Nothing that the Lord gives us to enjoy will satisfy us if this source of refreshment is not given. People of the world ask, *"Who will show us some good?"* (Psalm 4:6). The Christian forms his answer into a prayer, "Lord, make Your face shine on me." Let Your merciful kindness be my comfort. This gives the enjoyment of what is really good and supplies the place for imagined good. It is a blessing that never becomes nauseating, and will never end. Every fresh taste quenches the thirst for earthly pleasures. *"Everyone who drinks of this water"*—says our Savior—*"will be thirsty again, but whoever drinks of the water that I will give him will never be thirsty again"* (John 4:13-14). *"Delight yourself in the Lord, and he will give you the desires of your heart"* (Psalm 37:4).

The Source of Comfort

Do you wish to know this comfort? Then seek to approach God by the only way of access. Learn to see Him in the way in which a God of love is seen, *"in the face of Jesus Christ"* (2

Cor. 4:6). Guard against looking for comfort from any other source. Beware of that satisfaction in man-made wells that draw you away from the fountain of living waters. Let every day's refreshment be a step toward desiring and attaining renewed and sweeter refreshment for tomorrow.

Some people look at David's experience as if they could hardly expect to reach the same happiness, and so they go on in a low, depressed, and almost sullen state, refusing the privileges which are freely offered to them. This attitude is very dishonorable to God. Let them sincerely plead their interest in the word of promise—*"Remember your word to your servant"* (Psalm 119:49). Let them point out one or all of the promises of their God. Let them spread before the Lord His own handwriting and seals; and their Savior has said, *"According to your faith be it done to you"* (Matt. 9:29).

God Wants Us to Ask

God is willing that we should urge *"him strongly, saying, 'Stay with us'"* (Luke 24:29). Only the veil of unbelief stops us from seeing an unclouded, everlasting smile of merciful kindness on our heavenly Father's reconciled face. Let us see that He is the first, the habitual object of our thoughts, the satisfying well-spring of our delight—that He is the one desire to which every other is subordinate, and in which every other is absorbed.

Lord Jesus! I seek for a renewed enjoyment in Your merciful kindness. I do not want to forget that it was this that brought You down from heaven—that led You to endure the death of the cross—that has washed me in Your precious blood—that visits me with many loving signs of Your love. Oh, let all my days be spent in the sense of this merciful kindness for my comfort, and in giving to You the unworthy returns of grateful, devoted service.

Charles Bridges

(Grace Gems, n.d.-a)

Daily Reflections

Who does not want comfort? Our physical bodies and minds demand it and seek after it continually, but often in the wrong places. God offers us comfort for our souls. He may meet our physical needs, and many times does, but He is more concerned with our hearts.

1. What is the difference between patience and love in a trial, according to Bridges?
2. What does the comfort of God mean to you? Read Matthew 11:28.
3. What is meant by the prayer, *"Stay with us"*?

19

PSALM 42 - PRAYING IN DIFFICULTIES

*"Why are you cast down, O my soul,
and why are you in turmoil within me?
Hope in God; for I shall again praise him,
my salvation and my God"*
Psalm 42:11

The Dark, Cloudy Day

Believe in Him even when you are under a cloud, and wait for Him when there is no moonlight nor starlight. Faith's eyes that can see through rock can see through a gloom brought by God, and in it read His thoughts of love and peace. Hold tight to Jesus in the dark; surely you will see the salvation of God.

When Jesus hides Himself, carry on waiting, and pray loudly until He returns; it is not the time to be carelessly patient. I love to be saddened when He hides His smiles because I believe His love is patient, waiting, and believing in the dark. You must learn to swim and hold up your head above the water, even when the sense of His presence is not with you to hold up your chin.

The Hour of Temptation

I find my Lord going and coming many times a day. His visits are short, but they are both frequent and sweet. I can hear bad tales and difficult reports about Jesus from the Tempter (the devil) and my flesh, but love does not believe evil. I know that they are liars and that worry makes lies of Jesus' honest and unalterable love to me. Temptations that I thought were conquered and thrown down, rise again and revive themselves on me. I see that while I live, temptations will not die.

I find it to be very true that the greatest temptation out of hell is to live without temptations. Faith works best with the sharp winter storm in its face. Grace fades without difficulty. The devil is just God's master swordsman who is there to teach us to handle our weapons.

Self-Occupation

I am like someone who, traveling in the night, sees a ghost and sweats in fear, and does not want to mention it to his friend in case it increases fear.

I see many who think it is holiness to complain about things, and then do nothing; as if to say "I am sick" could cure them. They think complaints are a good charm for feeling guilty.

Let your bleeding soul and your sores be put in the hand of this expert doctor; let young and strong corruption and His free grace be yoked together, and let Jesus and your sins be dealt with between them. I do not want to put you off your fears, and your sense of deadness: I wish it were more. There are some wounds whose bleeding should not be stopped. Rather live close to the Doctor. It will be a miracle if you were the first sick person whom He did not cure, and were worse than when He found you. *"Whoever comes to me I will never cast out"* (John 6:37). Hold onto that. Faith is aware of sickness, and looking to Jesus, is glad to see His face. Christ is like a full feast when you are hungry. He is a miracle and a world's wonder to a seeking and crying sinner, but this miracle can only be seen by those who will come and see. The seeker and sigher will then become a singer and enjoyer.

You complain that you want a sign of the work of grace and love in your soul. For an answer, consider 1 John 3:14: *"We know that we have passed out of death into life."* And as for your complaint of deadness and doubtings, Jesus will take both your deadness and you together. They are bodies full of holes and broken bones which need mending that Jesus the Doctor can heal: whole vessels are not part of His work. Tax collectors, sinners, and prostitutes are what He is after. The only thing that will bring sinners close to Jesus' arm is some feeling of death and sin. A soul that is bleeding to death, until Jesus was sent for, and you cried for Him to come and stop the bleeding, and close up the wound with His own hand and ointment, is a very good disease when so many are dying with a whole heart.

Samuel Rutherford

(BibleTruth, n.d.)

Daily Reflections

Rutherford's style of writing is very personal, and this is probably because most of his work comes from letters that he wrote to other people. They not only give us an opportunity to relate but also to learn and grow in the insight that he provides.

1. Do you ever pray when it feels like God and heaven are clouded over? What kind of prayers do you say in these times?
2. What is Rutherford's view of temptation? How is this encouraging for us?
3. Are you someone who often complains about things? How does faith change the way we see these things?

20

PSALM 25 - LEARNING TO WAIT IN PRAYER

"Make me to know your ways, O Lord;
teach me your paths.
Lead me in your truth and teach me,
for you are the God of my salvation;
for you I wait all the day long"
Psalm 25:4-5

Think of an army about to enter an enemy's territories. Why would they wait? For supplies, instructions, or orders. If the last despatch had not been received, with the final orders of the commander-in-chief, the army dared not move. Even so in the Christian life, as deep as the need of waiting for supplies, is that of waiting for instructions.

See how beautifully this comes out in Psalm 25. The writer knew and loved God's law so much, and meditated on that law day and night. But he knew that this was not enough. He knew that for the right spiritual apprehension of the truth, and the right personal application of it to his own circumstances, he needed direct divine teaching.

The Psalm has always been a very strange one, because of its repetition of the need for Divine teaching, and of the childlike confidence that that teaching would be given. Study the Psalm until your heart is filled with the two thoughts—the absolute need and the absolute certainty of divine guidance. And with these, see how he speaks, *"For you I wait all the day long."* Waiting for guidance, waiting for instruction, all day is a very blessed part of waiting on God.

The Father in heaven is so interested in His children and longs to have our life at every step in His will and His love, that He is willing to guide us by His own hand. He knows so well that we are unable to do what is really holy and heavenly, except as He works it in us, that He means His very demands to become promises of what He will do, in watching over and leading us throughout the day. Not only in special difficulties and times of confusion but in everyday life, we can count on Him to teach us His way and show us His path.

And what do we need to receive this guidance? One thing: waiting for instructions, waiting on God. *"For you I wait all the day long."* In our times of prayer, we want to give clear expression to our needs, and our faith in His help. We want to become conscious of our ignorance as to what God's way may be, and the need for the Divine light shining within us, shining more and more like the perfect day.

And we want to wait quietly before God in prayer until the deep, restful assurance fills us: It will be given—*"The meek will he teach his way"* (Psalm 25:9 KJV).

"For you I wait all the day long." The special surrender to the Divine guidance in our seasons of prayer must cultivate, and be followed up by, the habitual looking upward *"all the day long."* As simple as it is, to one who has eyes, to walk all the day in the light of the sun, so simple and delightful it can become to a soul practiced in waiting on God, to walk all the day in the enjoyment of God's light and leading. There is only one thing necessary to help us to such a life: the real knowledge and faith of God as the one and only source of wisdom and goodness, always ready and longing to be to us all that we can possibly require. This is the one thing we need. If we could see God in His love, if we just believed that He waits to be gracious, that He waits to be our life and to work all in us—how this waiting on God would become our highest joy, the natural and spontaneous response of our hearts to His great love and glory!

"For God alone, O my soul, wait" (Psalm 62:5).

Andrew Murray

(World Invisible, n.d.)

Daily Reflections

Again, we find the topic of waiting. It seems to be one of the running themes all the way through the Psalms and is used about 20 times depending on translations. Mostly, it is used as a reminder or an encouragement to do so, probably because we find it so hard to do, or we forget to wait on God!

1. Why does Murray say we sometimes have to wait before entering in or receiving something?
2. What are the two things that are being waited for?
3. Murray says there is only one thing we need to get this right. What is it?

21

PSALM 84 - ONE DAY IN YOUR COURTS

"O Lord God of hosts, hear my prayer;
give ear, O God of Jacob! Selah
Behold our shield, O God;
look on the face of your anointed!
For a day in your courts is better
than a thousand elsewhere.
I would rather be a doorkeeper in the house of my God
than dwell in the tents of wickedness"
Psalm 84:8-10

If my strength was not in God, I would not dare to call on him, the Lord of hosts, but now that my strength is in him, and that I know he is Lord of Hosts for me, and not against me—a shield for me, a sword to my enemies—now I have the confidence to say, *"O Lord God of hosts, hear my prayer;*

give ear, O God of Jacob!" (v. 8). I do not doubt that he will hear me, even though he is the Lord of hosts, but I have much more confidence that he will listen to me, being the God of Jacob. He has made a covenant with Jacob and with his future generations forever, that he will be their God, and they shall be his people, and I am happy to be counted in that number. It is not because of the flesh, which profits nothing, but according to faith, the only thing that makes the true Israelite.

But what good will it do me that God hears my prayer and gives ear to it if he still opposes me and turns away his face? Therefore, *"Behold our shield, O God; look on the face of your anointed!"* (v. 9). I will never come to look on your face if you do not see fit to first look on mine. If you choose to not let your eyes look on me, as the favor of your ears to hear me, I will be left with nothing but an empty expectation of something that will never happen. But when you see fit to look on my face, that look of yours has an influence of true blessedness and brings me joy to have the God of Jacob as my shield.

But what if this prayer is just for David or for kings who, like David, are the Lord's anointed? What does it mean for us? It is true that kings are the Lord's anointed in a special manner, but every child of God is his anointed, too. Why else does it say that Jesus was anointed with the oil of gladness above his companions, (Psalm 45:7) if they (the children of God) were not also anointed? Anointed with the oil of grace is one thing, but to be anointed with the oil of gladness is the very thing I am praying for here, the very thing that makes me long for the courts of the Lord. *"For a day in your courts is better than a thousand elsewhere"* (v. 10).

It is not the length of time but the measure of joy that makes it wonderful, or maybe it is one day in God's courts that will never end that is better than a thousand days in this world that do end. If he had said, *"One day in his courts is as good as a thousand,"* which are huge odds of a thousand to one—there would have been some proportion. But he says, *"A day in your courts is better than a thousand,"* which seems to exceed all comparisons, and leaves no room for any proportion. One day in his courts gives possession of eternity, where a thousand that are spent anywhere else are but steps of mortality. If I had just one day in his courts, I would see what would be a joy to me all the days of my life, but if I spent a thousand in any other courts, I would see nothing but pride and worry.

As it is true for time, it is also true for place. *"I would rather be a doorkeeper in the house of my God than dwell in the tents of wickedness"* (v. 10). Is it so terrible to be a doorkeeper? The angel with the flaming sword was a doorkeeper to Paradise and Peter is the doorkeeper of heaven. What David is saying is that he would rather be Peter in the house of God than be Annas or Caiaphas in the court of Herod. If Jesus is the door, David would be content to be a doorkeeper. Even though there are many mansions in God's house, since they are all wonderful, even the doorkeeper's place is not without its glory. But if you think the role is worthless, think about who he serves. Even a doorkeeper serves in God's house, and God never moves his servants unless it is to promote them, but in the earthly courts, even the greatest officers are sometimes removed in disgrace.

This prayer not only shows the great glory of God's house, but the great humility of David's heart, and that he is not ambitious like the mother of Zebedee's sons, who saw no other place for her sons but to have one of them sit at his right hand, and the other at his left. Oh, gracious God, give me a doorkeeper's position in your house, that I may have the freedom to walk in thy house and to enjoy your presence where there is the fullness of joy forever more.

Richard Baker

(Baker, 1640)

Daily Reflections

Baker unpacks so much in this short passage that it almost needs another read-through just to catch everything that he is saying. From asking God to hear us, to acknowledging us, he ends with the idea of how wonderful it is to spend time in God's presence.

1. Why do you think God, the Lord of Hosts, takes time to listen and hear us? Do you sometimes feel like you are wasting His time with your prayers?
2. Why is the image of us "seeing God's face" and Him looking at us so important? What does it mean?
3. What does the image of a doorkeeper mean to you in this prayer?

22

PSALM 119 - NOT JUST A DUTY

"With my whole heart I cry; answer me, O Lord!
I will keep your statutes.
I call to you; save me,
that I may observe your testimonies"
Psalm 119:145-146

The whole heart is engaged in the cry. *"Save me"*—includes all the sinner's needs; pardon, acceptance, access, holiness, strength, comfort, heaven, all in one word—Christ. *"Save me"*—from myself, from Satan, from the world, from the curse of sin, from the judgment of God. This is the need for every moment to the end.

"I call to you"—What a mercy to know where to go! The way of access must have been implied in these short words. *"Save*

me"—through Him, whose name is Jesus the Savior. A moment's interruption of our view of Jesus brings a cloud across our way to God and paralyzes the spirit of prayer. Prayer is not only the sense of guilt and the cry of mercy, but the exercise of faith. When I come to God, I always bring with me the blood of Christ—my price—my plea in my hand. He cannot cast it out.

Here is the guarantee to believe that my God does, and will, hear me. Here is my encouragement to look up—to be watching at His gate like the cripple at the gate of the temple, expecting to receive something from Him. Not a word of this kind of prayer is lost. It is a seed—not scattered onto the earth, exposed to hazard and loss, but cast into the bosom of God, and here, as in the natural harvest, *"whoever sows bountifully will also reap bountifully"* (2 Cor. 9:6). Those who come frequently are the largest receivers—always wanting, always asking—living on what they have, but still hungering for more.

But for many, the ritual of prayer is everything, without any thought, desire, anxiety, or waiting for an answer. This only shows low thoughts of God and deep and guilty insensibility. But are God's children, who never used to miss the presence of God, seeking in tears, now too easily satisfied with the act of prayer, without the enjoyment of God? Perhaps you lament your deficiencies, your weakness in the hour of temptation, your indulgence of ease, your unfaithfulness of heart. But is your cry continually going up with your whole heart? Your soul would not be so empty of comfort if your mouth were not so empty of prayer.

We must not be content with keeping up the duty, without persistence in prayer in our duty. This will save us in times of temptation. Satan strikes at every Christian—unbelief quickly yields to his suggestions. This is the element in which we live—the warfare of every moment. Is morning and evening devotion enough in such an emergency? No. The Christian must *"take up the whole armor of God"* with unceasing *"prayer and supplication"* (Eph. 6:13, 18). If your heart is dead and cold, rather cry and wait as Luther used to do, until your heart is warm and woken up.

The hypocrite is satisfied with the barren performance of the duty. But the child of God, while he mourns, still holds on, even if only with tears, or *"groanings too deep for words"* (Rom. 8:26). Why is the believer so desperate for an audience?—why so restless in his cries for salvation? Is it not that he loves the statutes of his God; that he is grieved because of his inability to keep them; and that he longs for mercy, as the spring of his obedience? *"Answer me… I will keep your statutes… Save me, that I may observe your testimonies"*—evidence of an upright heart. Sin can have no fellowship with the statutes. As saved sinners, they are our delight.

Lord, You know how our hearts draw back from the spiritual work of prayer, and how we nourish our unbelief by our distance from You. Oh, pour on us this Spirit of grace and supplication. Teach us to pray—even our hearts, our whole hearts—to cry to You. Give us the privilege of real communion with You—the only satisfying joy of earth or heaven.

Charles Bridges

(Grace Gems, n.d.-a)

Daily Reflections

These questions and reflections are not meant to be adhered to strictly but are a means to open your mind to think a bit more personally about the issues raised, and to see where you stand in relation to them. Take your time, ask questions of your own, allow yourself to be vulnerable, and seek understanding for your own life.

1. Do you ever pray or cry to God with your "whole heart"?
2. Why does God love those who keep coming back and asking for more? Read 2 Cor. 9:6 again.
3. Are your prayers ever filled with *"groanings too deep for words"*? What does this mean? Why is the Holy Spirit needed for this?

23

PSALM 119 - PRIVATE PRAYER

"I rise before dawn and cry for help;
I hope in your words.
My eyes are awake before the watches of the night,
that I may meditate on your promise"
Psalm 119:147-148

The Psalmist does not just show us the passion but the seasons of his supplication. Like Daniel, he had set times of prayer, three times a day. But this was not enough as he waited all day on God. Prayer was indeed his meat, drink, and breath. *"I give myself to prayer"* (Psalm 109:4). Early and late he was found in the work of God; before sunrise for prayer, and again during the night watches, that he might meditate on the word. Look at Jesus: After a long busy Sabbath, when His body needed refreshment and rest, he still rose *"early in the morning, while it was still dark, he departed and went out to a desolate place, and there he prayed"* (Mark 1:35). On another occasion, *"all night he continued in prayer to God"* (Luke 6:12).

So long as the duty of prayer is all we know, we shall be content with our set times. But when the privilege is felt, we will be up early, following it closely morning and night. While family and social times are refreshing, it is the lonely, private communion with our God that produces our closest walk with God. Secret prayer is true prayer. There is no true prayer without it. It was the garden prayer—separate from His own disciples—that brought special support to the fainting humanity of Jesus. And if He needed this time, whose emotions were always fixed, what must our own need be, whose desires are so unstable! These were David's cries—penetrating no other ear but His Father's—delightful incense there.

David's Example

To see the King of Israel, with all His urgent responsibilities, making frequent daily times with the word of God and prayer—how does it expose the insincerity of our own excuse, that the pressing needs of the day allow no time for the service of God! It is not that we are busy and have no time for prayer, but that we are worldly and have no heart to pray. The consecrated heart will always find time for secret duties and will, like David, redeem it from sleep than lose it from prayer.

The night times and the dawn give us moments that are free from interruption when God expects to hear from us, and when the joy of fellowship with Him will be our strength for active service and our preservation from worldly traps. The thoughts of God were the first visitors to David's waking mind, and this was his habitual success in realizing His presence throughout the day. The lukewarmness and our lack of spiritual enjoyment can be traced to that morning laziness, which not only throws the business of the day into confusion but also consumes the time in self-indulgence or trifling, which should have been given to sacred communion. The effort made to overcome our flesh and deny the demands of the world is an exercise of self-denial, honorable to God. No memories of the past will be so refreshing in those last hours as the time made for communion with God.

And, even if there is no actual enjoyment, at least let us honor God by expectancy. I hoped in Your word. There can be no exercise of faith in the neglect of prayer; but the ground of faith, and that which gives to it life, hope, and joy, is the view of God in His word as a promising God. To hope in His word is to build up ourselves in our most holy faith and to lay all our desires, cares, weights, and burdens on a solid, unsinking foundation.

David's night watches were used in meditation in the word. Instability of faith comes from a lack of fixed recollection of the promises of God. This superficial habit may be enough for times of quietness, but during the winds of temptation, we can only have an anchor in habitual and intelligent confidence in the firm promise of the word. It needs to be the food of our meditation, and the ground of our support when our prayer seems to hang at the throne of grace without any sign of acceptance. Often, it will lift up our tired hands and supply fresh strength, and a wonderful victory. The ground is always solid with faith. May the Lord give us faith enough for our daily work, conflict, consolation, and establishment!

Charles Bridges

(Grace Gems, n.d.-a)

Daily Reflections

We often want to know when it is best to pray, what time, and for how long. This helps us to fit prayer into our own schedule and it becomes a set part of our day. But, there is more than this, as we can see in the Psalm. Times of prayer that are not scheduled or marked by time and place.

1. Do you have a set time for prayer every day? Why does this work for you?
2. Why is secret prayer so important to God?
3. Why is meditation on the word a useful and important part of prayer?
4. Read Matthew 6:6. Why does God reward this kind of prayer?

24

PSALM 6 - PATIENCE IN PRAYER

> *"O Lord, rebuke me not in your anger,*
> *nor discipline me in your wrath.*
> *Be gracious to me, O Lord, for I am languishing;*
> *heal me, O Lord, for my bones are troubled.*
> *My soul also is greatly troubled.*
> *But you, O Lord—how long?"*
> Psalm 6:1-3

David does not say, "How long before you hear me? If you hear me, how long before you answer me? If you answer me, how long before you heal me? How long shall my bones and my soul be troubled?" He continues to be patient and solicits the same God in the same name, "O LORD—how long?"

Do we need any other example of patience than God himself who waits so long in expectation of our conversion? But we have David's example too, who, having first asked God not to rebuke him in anger, then prayed that God would be patient with him. He is also content to wait on God for those other things which he asks until it is his pleasure to give them. But he does not stop praying or pray to anybody else.

Just as *"there is no other name under heaven given among men by which we must be saved"* (Acts 4:12), so there is no other name in heaven to receive these blessings but the name of Jehovah. Jehovah is the name of the whole Trinity, and there is no other, no queen-mother in heaven, no councilors in heaven in commission with the Trinity.

In this name, David pursues his prayer because a person can take lots of water at once from a river, but it will not be as pure as the water that comes from the fountainhead, the source.

Do not be in a rush to be rich—even in spiritual riches and spiritual health. Pray for it because there is no other way to get it. Desire to have these spiritual blessings, to desire them, is to begin to have them, but do not be in a rush. Do not think you are purer than you are, because you see someone else committing sins, as you once did. When Jesus comes with his judgment scales, you will not be weighed with that man, but every man will be weighed with God. Be pure as your Father in heaven is pure, is the weight that must judge us all.

Waiting as God Does

If you wrestle with temptations and cannot overcome them, if you pray sincerely and find your mind straying, if your intentions are good but you find obstacles on the way, do not be discouraged. God spent six days on his first work in creation before he came to make you, yet all that time, he labored for you. Your salvation, to make you a new creature, is a greater work than that, and it cannot be done in an instant. God has planned a work in you; he has sat down and considered that he has enough to accomplish that work, as it is in the Gospel, so let him do his work.

When you have begun as David did, with an *"O LORD, rebuke me not,"* and followed that with a *"heal me, O LORD,"* and find an *"O LORD—how long?"* arising in you, suppress it, overcome it, with more and more petitions. As God did by way of the commandment in the first creation, do in your prayer. First, he said, *"Let there be light"* (Gen. 1:3). So, pray that he will enlighten your darkness. God was satisfied with that light for three days, and then he said, *"Let there be lights"* (Gen. 1:14). So, bless God for his present light, but pray that he will enlarge that light which he has given you, and turn all those commandments into prayers, till you come to his *"Let us make man in our image"* (Gen. 1:26). Pray that he will restore his image in you, and conform you to him, who is the image of the invisible God, our Lord and Savior Christ Jesus.

He did his greatest work in you; before time began, you were chosen. He has reserved the completion of that work until time shall be no more, your glorification. As for your purpose, he has taken his own time, so wait for your sanctification, and if God has kindled some light in you, he may multiply this light by a more powerful means. If it is not soon, remember that it was God that made the sun stand still for Joshua, and he was glorified by that as much as when it moved. It is the same in your sanctification, though it seems to stand still for a time, when his time comes to perfect it, it will be acceptable to you. Nothing is acceptable to him, but that which is done in the right season. That is the nature of everything in which God has his hand in, so that is the time for everything, which God has appointed for it.

Pray and stay are two blessed words that will help us. To rise up to God, and to pay attention to God's work toward us, is the motion and the rest of a Christian. So, let all the motions of our soul in our prayers to God be that our will may rest in his and that all that pleases him may please us because it pleases him. Because it pleases him, it becomes good for us, and then, when it pleases him, it becomes seasonable to us and beneficial for us.

John Donne

(Bible Study Tools, n.d.)

Daily Reflections

Not only does Donne reveal some startling revelations here, but he also gives us practical tips to help us when we are struggling with having patience. By putting these small steps into practice, they can become our own and can assist us when we feel we are not able to wait on God any longer.

1. Is David not being impatient by asking God *"how long"*?
2. What are the three steps that Donne gives us when we are struggling?
3. What two words will help us? Do you find these easy to do?

25

PSALM 141 - GUARD MY TONGUE

"Set a guard, O Lord, over my mouth;
keep watch over the door of my lips!
Do not let my heart incline to any evil,
to busy myself with wicked deeds
in company with men who work iniquity,
and let me not eat of their delicacies!"
Psalm 141:3-4

"O Lord, I call upon you" (v. 1). From such a manner of praying, it is evident that David was not struggling through something small, as he repeats his requests and insists on receiving help. He teaches us by his example to pray immediately to God and not be tempted, as wicked men are, to renounce prayer and rely on other resources. He says that he cried to God, not to heaven or earth, to men or fortune, as the ungodly do. If they do address God, it is with complaints, howling rather than praying.

In the second verse, it sounds like a legal ceremony. At that time the prayers of God's people were according to his own appointment sanctified through the offering of incense and sacrifices, and David depended on this promise.

"Set a guard, O Lord, over my mouth." As David was liable to be hurt at the incredible rage of his enemies and might be tempted to act in a manner that might not be justifiable, he prays for godly direction, not that he might be kept back from violence, but that his tongue might be stopped from complaining or responding in anger. Even people who do not have a great temper, if injured without reason, will sometimes want to retaliate because they resent the behavior of their enemies.

David prays that his tongue might be restrained by the Lord from saying any word which was out of line. Next, he seeks that his heart will be kept from every mischievous thought that might end in revenge. The phrase—*"that I may not eat of their delicacies"*—is to be understood figuratively, as a petition that he might not be tempted by the prosperity that they enjoyed in sin and behave like them.

The three things mentioned in the context are to be connected, and we will consider each of them more closely. Nothing is more difficult than for the victims of unjust persecution to hold their tongues and submit silently and without complaint. David needed to pray that his mouth might be closed and guarded—that the door of his mouth might be kept shut by God, as one who keeps the gate watches the comings and goings—נצרה, nitsrah, being the verb, rather than a noun. He links that to God not letting his heart incline to an evil thing—דבר, dabar, is used to signify this. Immediately after that, he explains that he does not want to join with them in wickedness, and so become like his enemies.

In committing himself to the guidance of God, in thoughts and words, David acknowledges the need of the influence of the Spirit for the regulation of his tongue and of his mind, particularly when tempted by the insolence of his opposition. The tongue will slip unless it is continually watched and guarded by God, but there are also wrong emotions that need to be restrained. What a busy workshop the heart of man is, and there are so many schemes manufactured there every moment! If God does not watch over our heart and tongue, there will be no limits to the sinful words and thoughts that will come—what a rare gift of the Spirit is control of the tongue, while Satan is always making suggestions that can be quickly and easily agreed with, unless God prevents it.

It should not seem strange to speak about God inclining our hearts to evil, since it is in his hand to turn them to whatever he wills. Not that he prompts them to evil desires, but he surrenders the wicked over to Satan's tyranny; he is said to blind and harden them. The blame of our sins rests with us, and the lust which is in us. As we are carried to good or evil by our natural desire, it is not from any external impulse that they incline to what is evil, but spontaneously and of our own corruption.

By מנעמים, manammim, translated as delicacies, is the satisfaction felt by the ungodly when their sins are overlooked by divine tolerance. While their insolence becomes more brazen, even the Lord's people are in danger of being deceived by the prosperity they see them enjoying, and to take liberties themselves. So, David had a reason to pray for the secret restraints of the Holy Spirit, that he might be kept from feasting on their delicacies—being intoxicated into sinful pleasure through anything debasing, flattering, or agreeable in outward circumstances.

John Calvin

(CCEL, n.d.-a)

Daily Reflections

The tongue is both a wonderful and a terrible thing. From the mouth, we can bless and curse, so it is no surprise that this Psalm is a prayer for God to watch over and guard our mouths against saying what we should not say.

1. Have you ever been tempted to say something wrong? Are you able to pray in those moments and ask God for help?
2. Why is the Holy Spirit necessary in these times?
3. David does not just ask for help with his tongue. What else needs to be guarded so that they do not affect the tongue?
4. Read Proverbs 13:3 and Ephesians 4:29.

26

PSALM 124 - THANKSGIVING FOR BEING SAVED

*"Our help is in the name of the Lord,
who made heaven and earth"*
Psalm 124:8

This whole Psalm is alive with joy, the joy of an escape, of a triumph as wonderful as it was unexpected. The Babylonian beast has lost its prey, the Babylonian flood its victim, and the Babylonian hunter his prize. And yet it does not glory in his own strength, but in God. The Psalm gives the glory to God alone.

The first stanza opens with the confession, *"if it had not been the Lord who was on our side… then they would have swallowed us up alive"* (v. 2-3). The second stanza opens with a thanksgiving to Jehovah, who has not given them as prey to the teeth of their foes. And the whole Psalm closes and reaches its climax in the solemn credit—*"Our help is in the name of the Lord, who made heaven and earth."*

It is only because He who made all things, and who is ever making and ruling them, had once more surprised them with his power and goodness, that the captives escaped, and are once more praising God. It was good for them that they could rejoice in God. They had little else in which to rejoice. They were free, but were poor and weak, and troubled on every side. They returned to a land wasted by fire and sword, choked with jungle, overrun with wild beasts, and to a city that had been reduced to a heap of ruins.

God Saves and Protects

They had to watch against surprise attacks while they built. The fields, which they had cleared and plowed, were often plundered by marauding bands as the harvest approached. Yet these men spoke the words of this joyful and exultant Psalm! With brave hearts, they must have looked fortune, and misfortune, in the face! And if we ask the secret of their strength, the answer is plain and clear. It is simply this—trust in God. He had delivered them from the Babylonian snare, would He not sustain and guard them now that they had escaped? He had plucked them out of the dark tempestuous sea in which they were sinking; would He not give them rest from their enemies round about, and establish the work of their hands, now that they had returned to the city

He loved and were rebuilding the House in which He dwelt? Was it not reasonable to suppose that He had a purpose concerning them?

In their captivity, they had renounced the idolatry of their fathers. They had learned the first lesson of their law, *"Hear, O Israel: The LORD our God, the LORD is one"* (Deut. 6:4).

They had settled into an invincible faith in Him who had brought them through so many strange perils to the land and city they loved. He was their Savior, their Friend. And they were glad in Him *"who made heaven and earth"* and would be glad in Him. Whatever came, could not He, who made heaven and earth, defend them?

We, who have tasted that the Lord is good, should sing as sincerely and heartily as the Jews, *"if it had not been the Lord who was on our side… then the flood would have swept us away, the torrent would have gone over us; then over us would have gone the raging waters"* (v. 2-5). Should we not thankfully and joyfully declare that the Maker of heaven and earth has been, and is, and will be, our Help? In times of sorrow and confusion, nothing is more essential than that we should know that He who made all things, and rules all things, is our Refuge and Friend. With many forces, natural and political, over which we have no control, how can we carry a steadfast and composed heart unless we rest in the divine and tender Wisdom which orders all events and controls all forces to ends of righteousness and love?

God's will is your salvation; his aim is universal welfare. He has given you such guarantees and assurances of his goodwill toward you as the Hebrews did not and could not receive. In Jesus, He has both said, and shown, that He is love. If they could be joyful in Him, why can't you?

Are your sins worse than theirs? Are your troubles to be compared to theirs? Even if they are, there is forgiveness with God and salvation. They found peace, they rose to joy because they had learned to look away from their sins to Him whose *"love covers over a multitude of sins"* (1 Pet. 4:8). They had learned to see in the hardships a Divine discipline of correction and recovery. And there is no other hope for us. We must trust in the compassion of Him to whom we confess our iniquities, we must take the natural consequences as Divine corrections of our iniquities if we are to sing and give praise to the Lord our God.

Samuel Cox

(Cox, 1874)

Daily Reflections

Not all the Psalms are full of crying out for help and seeking God in times of trouble. Many of them are songs of joy and gratitude. We can learn a lot about how to thank God when we see these as responses to His goodness and faithfulness in our lives.

1. If you had to draw a graph for the amount of time you spent asking God for things versus thanking Him, which one would be higher? Is this surprising?

2. What reason did the Israelites have for being thankful? What reason do you have?
3. Are you able to thank God even in times of trouble? Read 1 Thessalonians 5:18.

27

PSALM 119 - THE WAY IS OPEN FOR PRAYER

"Let my cry come before you, O Lord;
give me understanding according to your word!
Let my plea come before you;
deliver me according to your word"
Psalm 119:169-170

The life of prayer is the cry of the heart to God. The eloquence of prayer is its sincerity. The power of prayer is not what comes from education or the natural desire of the man, but that which is from above—the spirit of supplication, *"the Spirit of adoption"* (Rom. 8:15). The urgency of present needs calls for immediate prayer. The soul is at stake; the enemy is within the walls. What a privilege to know that we can remind the Lord, *"You have given the command to save me, for you are my rock and my fortress"* (Psalm 71:3).

But we must see that our cry comes before—comes near—the Lord; that nothing blocks the way, or interrupts the communication. If we are believers, the way is open, the curtain has been torn. We should be encouraged to go nearer in communion, *"since we have confidence to enter the holy places by the blood of Jesus, by the new and living way that he opened for us through the curtain, that is, through his flesh"* (Heb. 10:19-20). Why should we not want to come?

If we had not seen the way marked by this blood, we should not have dared to take one step into the presence of God. We felt that we must pray or die, we should have had no boldness to open our mouths before God, much less to expect that our supplication would come near before Him, had we not been *"brought near by the blood of Christ"* (Eph. 2:13). But what a privilege it is, that this way to God is always open; that, as members of Christ, we stand in the sight of God as pure as Christ is pure; that we have not only access but access with confidence—the same confidence as the Son of God Himself!

But when we feel as if we could not reach the throne of grace, our distance from God must be traced to a deeper origin than the dullness and insensibility of our hearts. The real difficulty of prayer, the inability to pray, comes from an incorrect view of the way of access. All those that come in the name of Jesus are welcome. So, why should you not be welcome? The throne of grace was made for sinners such as you. You cannot want larger promises or a better plea. You come, not because you are worthy, but because you are told to come. Take the command and lay it on your conscience. Christ is your only way to God. Faith is the act and exercise of coming to Christ. Faith, therefore, will bring you to God, if you have not yet come; or will restore you to God, if you have wandered from Him.

Do we pray because we love to pray, or only because our consciences remind us to do the duty? Does the Lord mark those secret transactions with Himself, that show our hearts are really drawn to Him? Is it our soul's salvation that brings us to God? Are our services motivated by spiritual manifestations of Jesus? It is possible to continue for a long time in the outward ritual, and yet not one of our prayers comes before the Lord. We have not come in the appointed way and, therefore, we have not really come at all. Or if the name of Jesus has been attached to our prayers, it has just been a part of a formal system, not as dependent on seeking acceptance with God.

It is beautiful to observe the oil of the Psalmist's faith feeding the flame of his supplication. The promises were the breath of his supplication; motivating his expectation for a favorable answer, and exercising his patience until the answer should come.

Our Father even accepts the stammering language of faith in His children! As Luther says, "'Abba, Father' is but a cry, yet it does pierce the clouds that there is nothing else heard in heaven of God and His angels." Yet our loving Father understands us all. How much our Beloved enjoys communion with His people, *"which he obtained with his own blood"* (Acts 20:28).

Charles Bridges

(Grace Gems, n.d.-a)

Daily Reflections

Just the fact that we are able to pray to the Almighty God should be enough for us. Sometimes we take it for granted that God would even listen and allow the pitiful prayers of sinners to come before Him, but the way has been opened, and we are invited to come boldly before His throne.

1. How has the way been opened for our prayers to come before God?
2. How does Jesus' blood give us the confidence to come into God's presence?
3. How do we know that Jesus enjoys listening to us and spending time with us when we pray?

28

PSALM 28 - THANKS, DECLARATION, AND PETITION

"Blessed be the Lord!
For he has heard the voice of my pleas for mercy.
The Lord is my strength and my shield;
in him my heart trusts, and I am helped;
my heart exults,
and with my song I give thanks to him.
The Lord is the strength of his people;
he is the saving refuge of his anointed.
Oh, save your people and bless your heritage!
Be their shepherd and carry them forever"
Psalm 28:6-9

"*For he has heard the voice of my pleas for mercy.*" Real praise is established on sufficient and constraining reasons.

It is not irrational emotion but rises, like a pure spring, from the depths of experience.

Answered prayers should be acknowledged. How often do we fail in this duty? Would it not encourage others, and strengthen ourselves, if we faithfully recorded God's goodness, and made a point of exclaiming it with our tongue? God's mercy is not an inconsiderable thing that we can receive without so much as thanks. We should not put up with ingratitude and live daily in the heavenly atmosphere of thankful love.

Verse 7 shows David's declaration and confession of faith, coupled with testimony from his experience.

"The Lord is my strength." The Lord uses his power on our behalf and puts strength into us in our weakness. The Psalmist, by an act of appropriating faith, takes the omnipotence of Jehovah as his own. Dependence on the invisible God gives great independence of spirit, inspiring us with more than human confidence.

"And my shield." So, David found both a sword and shield in his God. The Lord preserves his people from countless troubles. The Christian warrior, sheltered behind his God, is safer than the hero that is covered with his shield of brass or triple steel.

"In him my heart trusts, and I am helped." Heart trust is never disappointed. Faith must come before help, but help will never be far behind it. Every day the believer may say, "I am helped," because God's assistance is given to us every moment, or we would go back to perdition. When more help

is needed, we have to put faith into exercise, and it will be given to us.

"My heart exults, and with my song I give thanks to him." The heart is mentioned twice to show the truth of his faith and his joy. The word exults means to "rejoice greatly"—we do not need to be afraid of rejoicing too much, remembering the grace we have received. We serve a great God, let us exult in him.

A prayer of thanks is the soul's best method of showing its happiness. It would be good if we were more like the singing lark, and less like the croaking raven. When the heart is glowing, the lips should not be silent. When God blesses us, we should bless him with all our hearts.

"The Lord is the strength of his people." The heavenly experience of one believer is a pattern of the life of all. To the whole church, without exception, Jehovah is the same as he was to his servant David—*"the feeblest among them on that day shall be like David"* (Zech. 12:8). We need the same aid and we shall have it, for we are loved with the same love, written in the same book of life, and one with the same anointed Head.

"He is the saving refuge of his anointed." Here we see king David as the type of our Lord Jesus, our covenant Head, our anointed Prince, through whom all blessings come to us. He has achieved full salvation for us, and we desire saving strength from him, and as we share in the anointing, which is so largely shed on him, we expect to partake of his salvation. Glory to the God and Father of our Lord Jesus Christ, who has magnified the power of his grace in his only begotten Son, whom he has anointed to be a Prince and a Savior to his people.

Verse 9 ends with a prayer for the church, written in short words but full of meaning. We must pray for the whole church, and not for ourselves alone.

"Save Your people." Deliver them from their enemies, preserve them from their sins, support them in their troubles, rescue them from their temptations, and ward off every evil from them.

"Bless your heritage." Give positive blessings, peace, plenty, prosperity, and happiness. Make all your purchased and precious heritage to be comforted by your Spirit. Revive, refresh, enlarge, and sanctify your redeemed people.

"Be their shepherd." Be a shepherd to your flock, let their physical and spiritual needs be plentifully supplied. By your word and commands, direct, rule, sustain, and satisfy those who are the sheep of your hand.

"And carry them forever." Carry them in your arms on earth, and then lift them into your bosom in Heaven! Elevate their minds and thoughts, spiritualize their affections, and make them heavenly, Christlike, and holy.

O Lord, answer this our petition, for Jesus' sake.

Charles Spurgeon

(Grace Gems, 2022)

Daily Reflections

This Psalm is a complete prayer with the many different facets all following each other from praise and gratitude to proclaiming God's attributes and finally asking for his continued protection and help.

1. What are you most thankful for, besides your physical needs being met? How often do you thank God for that?
2. Do you ever take time to tell God how mighty, wonderful, and great He is? Read Psalm 150:2.
3. How often do you pray for the church? Read Ephesians 6:18.

29

PSALM 17 - A PRAYER TO BE HEARD

"Hear a just cause, O Lord; attend to my cry!
Give ear to my prayer from lips free of deceit!"
Psalm 17:1

A prayer of David himself.

"*Hear a just cause, O Lord; attend to my cry! Give ear to my prayer from lips free of deceit!*" (v. 1)—not going up to You from deceitful lips. "*From your presence let my vindication come!*" (v. 2). From the enlightening of the knowledge of You, let me judge truth, that I may not in judging speak anything else than what I understand in You. "*Let your eyes behold the right!*"—the eyes of the heart.

"*You have tried my heart, you have visited me by night, You have tested me, and you will find nothing*" (v. 3). My heart has been proved by the tests and trials I have been given, not only the dark night but in the fire also; when I was examined, I was found righteous.

"I have purposed that my mouth will not transgress with regard to the works of man" (v. 3-4). That nothing may proceed out of my mouth, but only what relates to Your glory and praise; not to the works of men, which they do outside of Your will. Because of the words of Your peace, or of Your prophets, I have kept Your ways.

"My steps have held fast to your paths; my feet have not slipped" (v. 5). That the love of the church might be perfected in the straight and narrow ways that lead to Your rest. That I may still live forever in eternity, after accomplishing Your ways and have finished walking in Your paths.

"I call upon you, for you will answer me, O God" (v. 6). With a free and strong effort, I have directed my prayers to You so that I might have this power. *"Incline your ear to me; hear my words."* Do not let Your hearing bring me humiliation.

"Wondrously show your steadfast love" (v. 7). May Your blessings not be unappreciated so that they are not loved.

"Keep me as the apple of your eye" (v. 8)—which seems very small, and yet by it the sight of the eye is directed, and light is distinguished from the darkness; just as by Jesus' humanity, the divinity of the Judgment discerns between the righteous and sinners. *"Hide me in the shadow of your wings."* In the strength of Your love and mercy protect Me.

"He is like a lion eager to tear" (v. 12). My enemies have taken me like that adversary who *"prowls around like a roaring lion, seeking someone to devour"* (1 Peter 5:8).

"Arise, O Lord! Confront him, subdue him! Deliver my soul from the wicked" (v. 13). Come, God whom they think is asleep and does not care about sins, blind them in their own hate, that vengeance may prevent them from succeeding; cast them down. Not only will all this punishment happen to them, but also their memory has been filled with sins—darkness hidden from the light of Your truth, that they should forget God.

"As for me, I shall behold your face in righteousness when I awake, I shall be satisfied with your likeness" (v. 15). With their filthy and darkened hearts, they cannot see the light of wisdom and do not see me as You do. And when they have been satiated with their uncleanness, that they could not know me, I shall be satiated, when Your glory is shown in them that know me.

St. Augustine

(CCEL, n.d.-b)

Daily Reflections

It really helps to have portions of scripture broken down and explained verse by verse. This commentary style allows us to understand much more than we normally would just reading the Psalm through. St. Augustine unfolds rich meaning in each line.

1. Which part of this prayer speaks to you the most? Why?
2. Verse 6 is a confident statement of prayer. Are you able to say this? Read Jeremiah 33:3.
3. As in verse 15, the Bible often refers to seeing Jesus' face. Have you ever experienced this?

30

PSALM 119 - GRATITUDE FOR HIS GOODNESS

"You are good and do good"
Psalm 119:68

"*The goodness of God endureth continually*" (Psalm 52:1 KJV). The *'goodness'* of God refers to the perfection of His nature: "*God is light, and in him is no darkness at all*" (1 John 1:5). There is such an absolute perfection in God's nature and being that nothing is lacking or defective in it, and nothing can be added to it to make it better.

He is originally good, good of Himself; all creatures are good only by participation and communication from God. God is summum bonum, the highest good.

God is not only the Greatest of all beings but the Best. Any goodness in a creature has been given by the Creator, but

God's goodness is underived, for it is the essence of His eternal nature. He was eternally good before there was any communication of His fullness or any creature to whom it might be given. So, the first manifestation of this Divine perfection was in giving being to all things. *"You are good and do good"* (Psalm 119:68).

All that emanates from God—His decrees, creation, His laws, providences—cannot be anything but good: as it is written, *"And God saw everything that he had made, and behold, it was very good"* (Gen. 1:31). The 'goodness' of God is seen, first, in creation. Take the highest of God's earthly creatures, man. There is plenty of reason he has to say with the Psalmist, *"I praise you, for I am fearfully and wonderfully made. Wonderful are your works; my soul knows it very well"* (Psalm 139:14). Everything about the structure of our bodies attests the goodness of our Maker. How suited are our hands to perform their work! How good of the Lord to appoint sleep to refresh the tired body! How benevolent His provision to give our eyelids and brows for their protection!

The goodness of the Creator is not confined to man; it is exercised toward all His creatures. *"The eyes of all look to you, and you give them their food in due season. You open your hand; you satisfy the desire of every living thing"* (Psalm 145:15-16). Whether it is the birds, the animals, or the fish, abundant provision has been made to supply their every need. God *"gives food to all flesh, for his steadfast love endures forever"* (Psalm 136:25). Truly, *"the earth is full of the goodness of the Lord"* (Psalm 33:5 KJV).

God has not only given us senses, but also that which gratifies them; and this too reveals His goodness. Our physical lives could have been sustained without beautiful flowers for our eyes to see their colors, and our nostrils to smell their sweet perfumes. We could have walked the fields without our ears hearing the music of the birds. *"The Lord is good to all, and his mercy is over all that he has made"* (Psalm 145:9).

The goodness of God is seen when man transgressed the law of His Creator, but he held back his anger. He ushered in a regime of mercy and judgment. Would God be 'good' if He did not punish those who misused His blessings, abused His benevolence, and trampled His mercies beneath their feet? It will not be a reflection on God's goodness, but rather the brightest exemplification of it, when He will rid the earth of those who have broken His laws, defied His authority, mocked His messengers, scorned His Son, and persecuted those for whom He died.

The goodness of God is seen when He sent His Son: *"redeem those who were under the law, so that we might receive adoption as sons"* (Gal. 4:4-5). In the Gospel, the *"grace [which in Greek means benevolence or goodness] of God has appeared, bringing salvation for all people"* (Titus 2:11).

"Oh that men would praise the Lord for his goodness, and for his wonderful works to the children of men!" (Psalm 107:8 KJV). Gratitude is the return required from us who receive from His abundance, yet we do not give it simply because His goodness is so constant and so abundant because we experience it every day.

The goodness of God is the life of the believer's trust. It is this excellency in God that most appeals to our hearts. Because His goodness lasts forever, we should never be discouraged: *"The Lord is good, a stronghold in the day of trouble; he knows those who take refuge in him"* (Nahum 1:7).

When others behave badly to us, it should only motivate us to give thanks to the Lord more, because He is good; and when we are conscious that we are far from being good, we should bless Him because He is good. We must never tolerate a moment of unbelief about the goodness of the Lord; whatever else may be questioned, this is absolutely certain, that Jehovah is good; What He does and gives may vary, but His nature is always the same.

A. W. Pink

(The Reformed Reader, n.d.)

Daily Reflections

Sometimes we need to be reminded of the basics. We get caught up in the majesty and power of God, but we need to acknowledge that He is good. Not like a good child, but incredibly, inherently good, and it is all for our benefit.

1. Do you ever take time in prayer to tell God how good and wonderful He is?
2. Take some time and search how many times the words 'good' and 'goodness' appear in the Psalms in relation to praising God.
3. What does God's goodness mean to you?

31

PSALM 131 - PRAYING FOR HUMILITY

"O Lord, my heart is not lifted up;
my eyes are not raised too high;
I do not occupy myself with things
too great and too marvelous for me.
But I have calmed and quieted my soul,
like a weaned child with its mother;
like a weaned child is my soul within me"
Psalm 131:1-2

It is a prayer of humility, the honest words of a soul so childlike and humble that it can assert its own humility without losing it. To boast of one's modesty, or even to speak of it, is usually a sign that there is very little to boast about. But there is no boasting in this Psalm. Its tone is grateful, not self-seeking. It is an appeal to the great Searcher of Hearts about the real state of the heart that speaks to Him. It is a thankful acknowledgment that Jehovah has freed it from the agitations of self-will and brought it to the rest and peace of a constant trust in Him. And this theme is developed with rare skill.

It is this grace, this main and crowning virtue, to which David lays claim. To claim this virtue is to lose it, but David claims humility with humility. His words have no pride in them; they leave no impression of arrogance on us as we read them. We feel that he is alone with God; that he is showing God his heart as it really is; that he is thanking God for the meek and quiet spirit which He has given him.

This Psalm is full of beautiful expressions; for example, the description of pride suggested by the first verse—*"My heart is not lifted up; my eyes are not raised too high; I do not occupy myself with things too great and too marvelous for me."* So, pride has its seat in the heart, looks out from the eyes, and exercises itself in the daily walk and conversation.

"This pride," says David, "which takes possession of the whole man, has not been the animating and ruling spirit of my life. Lord, I have remembered that you live with those of a humble spirit, that you have respect for the lowly. So, if pride has crept into my heart, it has not found a home in my heart. If it has flashed from my eyes, I have not habitually walked with eyes lifted up in disrespect to others. If it has made me think about mysteries too great for my grasp, or to attempt enterprises beyond my strength, I have not habitually walked in the high, slippery places of thought or aimed too high for my own good.

I am content with normal thoughts, with the daily task of life, to search for what I could hope to know, to attempt what I could hope to do. I have not been reaching out to things which are beyond me, but have been content to learn the present truth, and to do the duty before me."

Humility Through Hardship

The second verse touches a higher, more poetic, chord—"*I have calmed and quieted my soul.*" The verb '*calmed*' is the same as that used by Isaiah when he speaks of leveling the ground after it has been turned up in clods by the plow (Isa. 28:25). It seems to imply that David had only gained peace through suffering; the plow of affliction had been driven back and forth on his soul before it was smoothed down. The use of the two verbs '*calmed*' and '*quieted*' implies and suggests the length and difficulty of the process. Not in a moment, not by a sudden and immediate effort, did he enter into rest.

In his soul, as in ours, there was long conflict. There were in his soul, as in ours, passions that longed after sinful gratification; mutinous powers of the will on which the yoke of the Divine law had to be painfully forced; eager desires for earthly good; and discontentment. All these had to be subdued, to be brought into harmony with reason and faith. The task was hard and long, the conflict severe. But at last, he succeeded in reducing and pacifying them; the warring and tumultuous passions of his soul subsided into stillness, and it lay calm and bright, like a lake untroubled by the wind. He had smoothed down and hushed his soul.

But David uses a more original and pathetic example than that of the lake. His soul, he says, lay on him *"like a weaned child with its mother."* Nothing can express the cost at which he found rest or the purity and unselfishness of the rest better than the image of a weaned child. A child is not weaned without lots of pain and strife. That familiar process is a child's first serious experience of loss, a pain that cannot be soothed, or a desire that cannot be gratified; here it meets its earliest demand for self-denial and self-control. But when the child is weaned, he lies still and content on his mother's chest, no longer craving and worried for his craving to be satisfied.

"So has it been with me," says David. "I was like someone banished from God, the source of all comfort and joy. I have had to endure pain, loss, and the stings of unsatisfied desire. But at last, my soul is weaned from all discontented thoughts, from all fretful desires for earthly good, from all selfish cravings, and waits in stillness on God, finding its satisfaction in his mere presence, resting peacefully in his arms." Or he speaks about his soul as apart from himself, lying in his own arms. Once it was restless and worried, a burden, exhausting him with its incessant demands, distracting him with its desires, but now, it has come back to him quiet, peaceful, gentle, and lies on him as the weaned child on its mother's breast.

A Secret to Learn

In these two verses David condenses the secret of his spiritual life; and, in the third verse, he asks the whole nation to learn that secret and live by it. Through a long, weary conflict with self-will and the impulses of passion and pride, he has entered into the peace of a humble and loving dependence on God. Let them also learn to wait on God and to hope in Him, and they will also be at rest. Weaned from self-will, from the passionate cravings and strife of a will opposed to Heaven, they shall rest in the calm, tender will of God and find all things working together for their good.

Our hearts are proud, and our eyes are lifted up. Too often, we focus on things too great and wonderful for us. And so, we are so restless and worried. There is no peace except in the humility which leans on God, trusts in Him, confesses weakness and ignorance and guilt, is not ashamed to say, "I do not know," and does not rejoice in the faults and defects of others, but rejoices in whatever is true, good, and kind. Only as we recover the spirit of a little weaned child and rest in simple, humble faith in God will we enter into the peace which passes all understanding.

Samuel Cox

(Cox, 1874)

Daily Reflections

Humility is a very hard attribute to acquire, and a difficult one to keep! That is why we need to ask God to help us, to give it to us, and lead us through situations where this character will be refined and worked in us.

1. Do you ever ask the Lord to humble you?
2. As David realized, humility comes through hardship that works our hearts. Do you ever ask for this, that you may gain humility?
3. What is David's spiritual secret?

ABOUT THE AUTHORS

St. Augustine

Referred to as one of the fathers of the Christian faith because of his views and writings, Augustine of Hippo was born in 354, a time when the Roman Empire was entering its last days. He was educated in philosophy and rhetoric, but was born again and baptized at the age of 31.

Although he served as a bishop for the ruling church at the time, many of his ideas and works on original sin and grace have been the foundation for many Reformists, especially Martin Luther.

His most well-known works, *On the Trinity* and *On Free Choice of the Will*, continue to be a reference point to this day for many prominent Christian writers and preachers.

Richard Baker

Born in 1568 in Kent, England, Baker attended university and worked his way into parliament, where he was elected as a representative. King James I knighted him in 1603, and he became high sheriff at Oxfordshire.

When he married, he took on the debt of his wife's family, which resulted in him losing everything and being thrown into prison, where he remained until he died in 1644.

It was during his confinement in Fleet Prison that he began writing some of his best-known works. His most famous was a historical account of the Royal monarchs' lineage, but he also produced meditations on the Lord's Prayer, Psalms, and Prayer.

Charles Bridges

Charles Bridges was part of the leadership of the Evangelical party in the Church of England. A very popular preacher who shared the pulpit with J. C. Ryle, he is more well-known for the books and writings that he produced.

Ordained in 1817, he served as vicar in Suffolk and then later in Dorset. During this time, he penned expositions on Psalms, Proverbs, and Ecclesiastes, among others, and his books were highly regarded by Charles Spurgeon.

Bridges died in 1869, leaving behind a rich deposit of Christian literature that has, and continues to, impact many believers in their understanding of the Bible and their walk with the Lord.

John Calvin

Calvin is probably most well-known for his formation of theological thinking that became known as Calvinism.

Trained as a lawyer, Calvin left the Catholic Church and joined the Protestants, finally moving from France to Switzerland, where much of his preaching and writing was done. His views were not always well received by those in power, and he was expelled and resited on many occasions.

Despite the controversy he generated, Calvin continued his tireless promotion of the Reformation until he died in 1564. He wrote many biblical commentaries and other works, although his *Institutes of the Christian Religion* remains his most familiar book.

Samuel Cox

Cox was born in 1826 in England and became a Baptist minister at the age of 26. A throat condition prevented him from preaching anymore and he turned his attention to writing. He produced a number of his own works but was also an editor for religious periodicals. When his voice healed enough, he continued to preach and became president of the Baptist Association in 1873. He retired a few years later and died in 1893.

Cox wrote 30 volumes ranging from biblical commentaries and expositions to arguments on miracles. His magazine was very popular, and with a dedicated team, they expounded scriptural views which shaped many doctrinal views of the day.

John Donne

Donne is probably best known as a poet, whose works continue to be read, quoted, and used in English due to their metaphorical and sensual style. But he also became a cleric, and his sermons were just as highly regarded in Christian circles as his poetry was.

A well-educated man, Donne lived off his friends for most of his early life, having squandered what he had from his inheritance on worldly pleasures. In 1615, he became an Anglican priest and held different positions, even Dean of St. Paul's.

Donne's work shows a significant change from the more sensual poetry to somber religious writing that dominated his later life until his death in 1631.

Jonathan Edwards

Edwards was a revivalist preacher during the early 1700s. Interested in natural science and the scriptures from an early age, his work shows an educated, argumentative style that is analytical.

After his education had finished at Yale University, he became a pastor and continued to study, but this time, his focus was on conversion and its process. This gave Edwards a clear understanding of the necessity for people to hear the Gospel and be truly born again, which would form the basis of his revivals.

His most famous sermon, *Sinners in the Hands of an Angry God*, displays his direct, no-nonsense approach that pervades all his writing, as does his book entitled *Religious Affections*.

Matthew Henry

The name Matthew Henry is synonymous with commentaries on the Bible, and his six-volume work on the scriptures remains the most referred-to writings by pastors, preachers, and authors.

Born in 1662, Henry could read the Latin and Greek New Testament by the age of nine. He was ordained as a Nonconformist minister in 1687 and began preaching in Chester and other churches in the area. Although his sermons were popular, using an expository style, his health prevented him from preaching as much as he wanted.

Despite this, he continued to travel and deliver sermons, as well as work on his commentary of the New Testament. While riding to another engagement, he fell off his horse, and the injury he sustained resulted in his death in 1714.

Andrew Murray

The son of a Scottish Dutch Reformed minister, Murray grew up in South Africa. He received his education in Scotland, where he met William Burns and was influenced by the revivals he witnessed there.

In 1856, he married and, although he settled as a minister of a church, he became known for his preaching and insight into the Bible. Invitations to travel to other countries began pouring in, and he soon found himself busy across the globe. In addition, he headed up missionary training institutes and unions that could serve others who were spreading the Gospel.

At the time of his death in 1917, Murray's work had become recognized in many countries, especially his books which, apart from their beautiful style of writing, were filled with incredible perception.

A. W. Pink

Arthur Walkington Pink's work began in the early 1900s and sparked a renewed interest in Calvinism and Reformed Theology.

Born in England in 1886, Pink was part of an occult gnostic group, but he left this when he turned to Christianity in 1908. Moving to the States, Pink studied at the Moody Bible Institute before moving to a number of different congregations. He died in 1952, having been shunned by certain churches because of his style and doctrinal beliefs.

A controversial writer, Pink's views showed significant changes as he himself was learning and understanding the Gospel more and more. His later years were spent almost exclusively on his books, and he produced a number of publications, which became even more famous after he passed away.

Samuel Rutherford

A Scottish Presbyterian minister, Rutherford is known for his letters that he wrote to challenge and encourage people. These were filled with incredible insight as well as a personal understanding of the scriptures.

Born in 1600, Rutherford was well educated but had significant run-ins with the order of the day because of his Nonconformist views. After the Restoration, his was one of the first works to be publicly burned, and he was charged with treason but died in 1661 before he could be tried.

He wrote prolifically and his letters were esteemed by many as much as books and other publications of the day, including Charles Spurgeon.

Richard Sibbes

Sibbes was an Anglican theologian born in 1577. He was well educated and became a lecturer at Holy Trinity Church, Cambridge. Following the beliefs of Puritanism, he was involved in providing support for other preachers and instituted groups to help fund and see that men could carry on the work of the Gospel.

Sibbes wrote many books covering numerous topics as well as having a series of his own sermons published. At the time of his death in 1635, he was 58 years old and was esteemed by many of his colleagues, having been given a Doctorate in Divinity.

Charles Spurgeon

Charles H. Spurgeon was a renowned Christian writer from the mid-1800s who had a way with words, both in his preaching and writing. Affectionately known as the "Prince of Preachers" for his eloquence and use of dramatic stories in his sermons, he was either criticized for his style or loved.

Born again at the age of 15, he went on to preach all over England and soon had the largest congregation, numbering 5,000. He was known to tackle issues head-on and was never afraid to proclaim the Gospel with his straightforward approach.

His health deteriorated in his late 30s, and Spurgeon had to retire from active preaching until his death in 1892.

R. A. Torrey

Reuben Archer Torrey was born in 1856 and enjoyed his days at Yale University as an academic. But toward the end of his time there, at the brink of suicide, he turned to God and became a preacher.

Instead of becoming critical of issues and the Bible, he saw the importance of fundamental foundations to be taught and defended. Torrey traveled across the world preaching and evangelizing as well as fulfilling the role of pastor, mission superintendent, and dean of a Bible college.

He wrote over 40 books, many of which are still regarded as classics in doctrinal teaching. Remembered as a man who "prayed it through" in every situation, Torrey died in 1928.

Thomas Watson

Born in 1620, England, Watson was known for his intense studying while at college, and his love for knowledge and understanding shows in the many books that he wrote.

As a Puritan preacher, he was briefly imprisoned because of his strong Presbyterian views during the civil war. Despite being reinstated as vicar on his release, his popularity as a preacher found him on the wrong side of the law again when the Restoration ejected him from the church because of Nonconformity.

Watson continued his work privately when he could, writing as much as possible until his health took a turn for the worst. He died suddenly during a moment of personal prayer in 1686.

BIBLIOGRAPHY

Baker, R. (1640). *Meditations and Disquisitions upon the first Psalme of David, etc.].* Edward Griffin, For Francis Eglesfield.

Bible Study Tools. (n.d.). *Sermon XLIX, The Works of John Donne Volume 2.* Biblestudytools.com. Retrieved August 15, 2022, from https://www.biblestudytools.com/classics/the-works-of-john-donne-vol-2/sermon-xlix.html

BibleTruth. (n.d.). *2. The Troubled Soul - Samuel J. Rutherford (#161713) - Bible Truth Library.* Bibletruthpublishers.com. Retrieved August 7, 2022, from https://bibletruthpublishers.com/2-the-troubled-soul/samuel-j-rutherford/letters-of-samuel-rutherford/s-rutherford/la161713

CCEL. (n.d.-a). *John Calvin.* Ccel.org. Retrieved August 12, 2022, from https://ccel.org/ccel/calvin/

CCEL. (n.d.-b). *Philip Schaff: NPNF1-08. St. Augustine: Exposition on the Book of Psalms - Christian Classics Ethereal Library.* Ccel.org. https://ccel.org/ccel/schaff/npnf108/npnf108.ii.XVII.html

Chapel Library. (n.d.). *The Acceptable Sacrifice.* Retrieved August 7, 2022, from https://www.chapellibrary.org/api/books/download?code=buasac&format=pdf

Christianity.com. (n.d.). *Psalm 20 Bible Commentary - Matthew Henry (complete).* Www.christianity.com. Retrieved August 8, 2022, from https://www.christianity.com/bible/commentary/matthew-henry-complete/psalm/20

Cox, S. (1874). *The Pilgrim Psalms.* Daldy, Isbister & Co. https://archive.org/details/pilgrimpsalmsan00cox-goog/page/n4/mode/2up?view=theater (Original work published 1874)

Crossway. (2001). *English Standard Version Bible.* Crossway Bibles.

Grace Gems. (n.d.-a). *Bridges Psalm 119.* Gracegems.org. Retrieved August 9, 2022, from https://gracegems.org/26/Bridges_psalm_119.htm

Grace Gems. (n.d.-b). *His Heart Is Fixed.* Www.gracegems.org. Retrieved August 7, 2022, from https://www.gracegems.org/Watson/his_heart_is_fixed.htm

Grace Gems. (2022). *The Treasury of David.* Gracegems.org. https://www.gracegems.org/Spurgeon/Treasury%20of%20David.htm

Monergism. (n.d.). *Edwards-Divine Sovereignity.* Retrieved August 12, 2022, from https://www.monergism.com/thethreshold/sdg/pdf/edwards_divinesovereignty.pdf

Mullers. (n.d.). *Müllers | Bringing Christian Hope and Wholeness to Children and Young People since 1834*. Www.mullers.org. Retrieved August 10, 2022, from https://www.mullers.org/mullerssermons

Murray, A. (2015). *Have mercy upon me: the prayer of the penitent in Psalm 51 explained and applied*. Ichthus Publications. https://archive.org/details/havemercyuponme00murrgoog/page/n122/mode/2up

The Highway. (n.d.). *A Breathing After God by Richard Sibbes*. Www.the-Highway.com. Retrieved August 10, 2022, from https://www.the-highway.com/Sibbes_A_Breathing_After_God.html

The Reformed Reader. (n.d.). *Attributes of God, The Goodness of God, Arthur W. Pink*. Www.reformedreader.org. Retrieved August 16, 2022, from http://www.reformedreader.org/aog03.htm

Thomas Nelson Publishers. (2014). *Holy bible, KJV.* Thomas Nelson Pub.

Torrey, R. A. (1915). *Shepherd Psalm*. Biola Publications. https://digitalcommons.biola.edu/biola-pubs/17

World Invisible. (n.d.). *Waiting on God*. Www.worldinvisible.com. Retrieved August 7, 2022, from https://www.worldinvisible.com/library/murray/waiting/waiting.htm

www.ingramcontent.com/pod-product-compliance
Lightning Source LLC
LaVergne TN
LVHW010221070526
838199LV00062B/4681